THE VASA. THE ROYAL SHIP

Lars-Åke Kvarning
Bengt Ohrelius

THE VASA
The Royal Ship

Translated by Joan Tate

ATLANTIS

Atlantis, Stockholm
© *Lars-Åke Kvarning and Bengt Ohrelius*
1972, 1978, 1990, 1998
© *Bokförlaget Atlantis* AB *1998*
Graphic Design: Christer Jonson
Jacket illustration: Tim Tompson
Reprinted 2002
Printed and bound by Graphicom Srl, Italy 2002
ISBN 91-7486-581-1

If not otherwise stated the pictures have been taken by
the photographers of the Wasanämnden (The Wasa Council)
and the Swedish National Maritime Museum.

Anders Franzén, p. 50, 56, 60, 63, 99a;
Hans Hammarskiöld, p. 111, 114, 115, 118, 119,
127, 142, 161b, 168, 169, 171; Björn Hedin, p. 78a;
Lennart Herlin, p. 19, 129; Ola Husberg, p. 172–173;
Gunnel Ilonen, p. 149, 165; Jahn Mörrby, p. 108;
Rolf Petterson, p. 162; Göran Sallstedt, p. 80;
Richard Tiefenbacher, p. 153.

CONTENTS

Anders Franzén searched for the Vasa with grappling-irons and plummets, work which tried his patience but produced results in 1956.

Per Edvin Fälting – head diver and key figure in the salvaging of the Vasa.

Foreword

FORTY YEARS will soon have gone by since the first version of this book was published in 1959. It was written just before the final stage of the salvage operation and while everything surrounding the event was marked by the drama and pioneer spirit of the excitement of the unknown. A great many colourful and skilled professionals carried out the salvaging project with confidence and indefatigable energy. First to be mentioned here is Anders Franzén, the originator of the Vasa project, but also Axel Hedberg, a leading figure as the salvage captain, Per Edvin Fälting the chief diver, and the chief archaeologist, Per Lundström, later Director of the National Maritime Museum – all of whom have since died, as has Bengt Ohrelius, who wrote the first version of this book.

The years following the inauguration of the Wasa Shipyard in 1962 have not been marked by the same drama prevailing during the salvaging stage, but as far as the Vasa is concerned, they have certainly been eventful. The old wreck has again become a ship to which its former splendour has been restored. Preservation, restoration, fund raising and then carrying out the construction of the permanent Vasa Museum have required major contributions from all those involved. Difficult solutions to problems have occasionally sent minds surging and the waves of discussion have been very high. But most things have been solved amicably and great national as well as international interest has also provided equally much stimulus to the work.

With a starting point in what happened during the hectic salvaging years, this book is intended to provide a coherent picture of what has happened to and around the Vasa, the oldest, fully identified salvaged and now restored ship in the world, which on December 6th, 1988 made her last voyage into the building in which she is to rest in future.

In 1989, a controversial old issue was settled with regard to the Vasa. In a press statement from the Wasa Shipyard, it was stated that: »the famous warship is being re-spelt: Wasa becomes Vasa«. This orthographic reform was carried out after a decision by the museum board, which stated: »from now on the museum will spell the warship Vasa with a V. Thus the Vasa Museum also becomes the correct spelling for the new copper-clad building now completed in Djurdgården«. This resolution has, of course, been accepted in this book, which means that there may appear to be some inconsistencies.

Stockholm, March, 1998
LARS-ÅKE KVARNING

The *Saint Louis* alias the *Vaisseau du Roi*, alias the *Royal*.
French warship built in Holland in 1626.
She may have served as a model for the Vasa, which, however, was larger.

LOST SHIPS

THE TIME MACHINE is a fascinating product of human imagination, perhaps an absurdity. Perhaps people will one day be able to journey into time, for curiosity and the thirst for knowledge are powerful driving forces. But fortunately, journeys into time can be made without the help of machines, and the unique find of the Vasa in the waters of Stockholm is good testimony to that. The old ship, which rested in her dismal grave off Beckholmen in Stockholm harbour at a depth of thirty-two metres for over three hundred and thirty years, has stimulated a number of scholars to focus their interest on the seventeenth century way of life. Over a long period of time, forgotten documents on the disaster have been retrieved from the archives and published. Hundreds of thousands of tourists make pilgrimages every year to admire this remarkable ancient ship.

Purposeful research enthusiasm, imagination and interest in maritime history in one man has provided the historians with a chance of acquiring a truer picture of Swedish standards of living at sea, naval life, the art of shipbuilding and much more in the seventeenth century. The story behind the find is considerably longer and perhaps more exciting than the ship's own brief life. A benevolent fate and the private scholar Anders Franzén have saved this singular ship from annihilation for posterity.

In the Baltic Sea, in our time sometimes called the »sea of peace«, the fleets of the great powers have fought a life and death battle. On several occasions in storm and rough seas, great warships have been wrecked on shallow coasts, where they have foundered, or during battle, when they have gone down with flags flying, defeated by superior opponents.

9

As long ago as in the 1930's, the man behind the find of the Vasa, Anders Franzén, had found that the Baltic had all the prerequisites for becoming an eldorado for maritime researchers. Its waters were lenient to the many sunken ships, as the ship-worm, *Teredo Navalis*, and similar damaging organisms, do not like the brackish waters of this inland sea. From the archives, Franzén then selected some Swedish naval ships of the sixteenth and seventeenth century, i.e. the period before ship's drawings came into use – ships that were lost with all on board. His Majesty's fleet was more generously armed and manned than the small anonymous and undermanned merchant ships of the day.

The seabed is an extensive field to work in and difficult to cover, requiring special working methods, special tools and great patience. When the scuba diver came into being in the 1950's, it was possible seriously to systematise underwater archaeology. Versatile electronic equipment, television cameras etc. have successively made this even more effective.

However, the marine archaeologist would never have got so far had he devoted all his time to underwater work. An essential part of the work had to be carried out on land. The scholar perhaps finds a clue in the literature of the history of warfare at sea. Then it is a matter of indefatigably and vigilantly following the trail with advanced detective work. Valuable information on sunken ships is found in the bulky volumes of archives. With luck and patience, and if the researcher is sufficiently skilled, it is perhaps possible with the help of old documents to reconstruct dramatic shipwrecks which occurred several centuries ago. State Councillors have perhaps written a report to the king in the field. Another possibility is that leading private individuals have investigated the loss of a large naval ship. Perhaps the loss once gave rise to extensive investigations and enquiries, and records of old trials can provide a great deal of information. A great deal can also be found in the annals of the Navy, in bills and other documents needed to complete the picture of the course of events of a lost ship, its crew and equipment. Then it becomes a matter of completing the puzzle and turning the pieces into a whole picture.

Usually it is very difficult, if not to say impossible, to extract from old records the exact position of a wreck. The last valuable lead may come in the form of a notice in the press saying that a fisherman has his equipment caught in something, and it had been ruined by some mysterious object on the seabed somewhere near the presumed site of the accident. A trip to the spot can practically always provide some valuable information. Stories about accidents at sea are often handed down through the centuries. The priest on the spot has perhaps had something to say, church records often contain information of importance, and a lead may even be

**This childhood portrait of Queen Kristina
in the 1630's was probably painted by
J.H. Elbfas. The naval yard at Gamla
Skeppsholmen (nowadays Blasieholmen)
can be seen through the palace window, the
warships made fast with the stern facing
land. Detail of painting.**
National Portrait Collection at Gripsholm.

**Gustav II Adolf, King of Sweden
1611–1632, had the Vasa built.**
National Portrait Collection at Gripsholm.

found on a gravestone in some corner of a hidden-away churchyard. Conversations and interviews may provide the last essential piece of the puzzle, and occasionally hints about old disabled ships and sites of accidents are found on sea charts.

Anders Franzén devoted his special interest to a great many ships, all of which cannot be described here, but it is tempting to flavour the names of the ships. *Resande Man* (Travelling Man) is a small 22-cannon ship. It sank in a storm in the late autumn of 1660, somewhere near Landsort, with a valuable cargo of gold and silver ojects on board. The ship was on its way to Poland with the diplomat, soldier and adventurer, Carl Christopher von Schlippenbach. The *Resande Man* was on urgent business. Schlippenbach had succeeded in interesting the regency of King Karl XI in an alliance with Poland against Russia. With expensive gifts, this intriguer and adventurer was now also to attempt to interest the Polish Prince Johan Kasimir in his cause. The expedition ended unhappily and Schlippenbach himself lost his life when the *Resande Man* went down. Her guns, anchor, hawsers and sails were salvaged in the summer of 1661. The salvage operation also managed to bring up some caskets of coins, but then the wreck was forgotten and its exact position remained a secret.

One summer's day in 1920, a fisherman found his anchor caught on something on the seabed off the island of Viksten, quite close to Landsort. By chance, a salvage craft with divers on it happened to be nearby. The fisherman asked the diver to go down and free the anchor for him. It turned out that the anchor had caught on an old wreck. This was identified later by the leading expert on King Gustaf II Adolf, Professor Nils Ahnlund, as the wreck of the man-of-war *Riksnyckeln* [Key of the Realm]. That ship was lost in 1628 on her way home from Germany from where she was carrying wounded men. This time, sheer chance provided the nation with seven handsome guns, now in the Maritime Museum in Stockholm.

Right in the middle of the fairway of Mysingefjärden, in deep water in the southern archipelago of Stockholm, lies King Johan III's proud ship the *Lybska Örn* [The Lübeck Eagle], which sank in 1576. The ship had 33 iron guns and 23 bronze guns. Nothing is known about how the loss occurred. Nor is it known where exactly the ship lies, but it is possible that Örngrundet outside Nynäshamn was once the fate of the *Lybska Örn*.

During the days of sailing ships, Dalarö was Stockholm's outer harbour. The king and his representatives often went there to discuss matters with admirals or to embark on one of the warships. But ships have been lost even in the sheltered harbour of Dalarö. In the summer of 1676, the man-of-war *Riksäpplet* [Apple of the Realm] was wrecked in a south-westerly storm on a small skerry and sank at sixteen metres depth. The little islet is today still called Äppelskär [Apple Skerry]. The *Riksäpplet* had a crew of 500 men and carried 86 guns.

Yet another ship was lost in Dalarö harbour. The same year as the *Riksäpplet* sank, the *Gröne Jägaren* [the Green Hunter] blew up and sank to the depth of thirty metres.

One of the ships in Sweden's first regular navy, purchased from Germany by King Gustav Vasa, has lain sunk in Nämndöfjärden since 1525, at a depth of thirty metres just north of Dalarö. She sank with a great many men on board and had also contained spoils of war taken from the Danes.

Inside Nybroviken in Stockholm lies the 44-gun ship *Västervik*. She caught fire and sank there during the 1676 year of misfortune, when Sweden also lost the sea battle against the Danish-Dutch fleet at Öland. In dramatic circumstances, the great ship *Kronan* [the Crown] was lost with 850 men on board. This ship was also found by Anders Franzén and his collaborators.

However, the most sensational of all wrecks found off the coasts of Sweden is that of the Vasa, which sank on her maiden voyage in 1628 in the Stockholm harbour area. Anders Franzén had his original inspiration for his researches from Professor Nils Ahnlund. When he had established the identity of the *Riksnyckeln* in 1920, at the same time Ahnlund found and published material on the Vasa, a contemporary.

This clearly spurred on Franzén's researches. He looked up in books, searched archives, compared and sorted information, as well as finally trying to establish the exact position of the wreck. In the spring of 1954, he had come so far that he knew the wreck ought to lie somewhere between Beckholmen and Södermalm. The National Council's report to King Gustaf II Adolf on the disaster was what finally provided Franzén with the right leads and persuaded him to move his investigations to the right area.

Busy shipping in the actual fairway often constituted serious elements, and the relatively large depth to the seabed made the work much more difficult. But the site also had clear advantages to offer. Strömmen was a place to work where it was sheltered from the weather, and with the help of the city churches and other dominating buildings, it was easier to acquire safe sight lines to localise suspected finds.

Examination of the seabed was a thorough and very time-consuming procedure without access to modern electronic aids. This was done by sweeping with steel wires and by using grappling irons and sounding equipment. Within the actual area were a great many underwater cables, so the dragging had to be done with great care. The situation of every find was carefully decided through sight lines. In all suspected places, attempts were made with a special plummet with a core sampler on the end in order, if possible, to try to pick up a specimen of timber.

Anders Franzén has himself written the following on his laborious work:

»What has been a great help has been the detailed map drawn up by Stockholm City in co-operation with the projection of the suggested Österleden.

»The actual area in this context has been echo-sounded with great precision, and sediment samples have been taken from the seabed right down to the basic rock, which in the deepest places is 60 metres below the surface of the water.

»If you carefully study the contours of the seabed on this map, you find a marked rise in the seabed outside the Gustav V dock, just where the Vasa turned out to be. Experts I consulted told me that this sediment consists of stone that had been blasted when the dock was being constructed. So as not to lose any more grappling irons and leads, I unfortunately avoided this area right up until 1956, when from another quarter I found that all the material from the building of the dock had been used to fill in Beckholmen's inner point. I still did not realise that this was the Vasa.

»Although the Vasa had lain on the seabed for 326 years, I considered I should now hasten the search, as the City Council had decided that the stone-tipping planned for Riddarfjärden was to be redirected to this area.

»The following relatively safe indications had been crystalised by the summer of 1956:

1. 30 metres depth (18 fathoms with correction for sediment and secular rise in the seabed)

2. 'Opposite Tegil-wijken'

3. 'Bleekholmsudden'

»The latter name cannot be verified by Stockholm City Museum, but is presumed to be identical with the then not yet filled in Beckholmsudden. A number of researchers have interpreted the name to Blockhusudden.

»On the above mentioned special map, I shaded in all the areas of about 30 metres depth south of Beckholmen. Some information now pointed to the rise in the seabed outside the GV dock, and when in August 1956 I succeeded in bringing up a piece of black oak in this place, I considered I could suggest to the relevant people at the Naval Dockyard to locate the recurrent annual testing of divers to this place. The divers soon found the wreck of the Vasa.«

As early as on this occasion, Franzén received great help from the man who was to hold a key position in the salvaging of the Vasa – the head diver, Per Edvin Fälting. He was also the first, in September 1956, to go down to examine the find.

In one blow, the find of the warship Vasa made Anders Franzén world-famous. He appeared on television, spoke on the radio, appeared in newspapers and magazines all over the world. Nowadays his name can be found in most marine-archaeological works of any importance. In all the Vasa exhibitions and films that have circulated all over the world, his contributions are mentioned. Over the years, Anders Franzén himself has appeared in many contexts and talked about his find. He has been awarded an honorary doctorate by two American universities, and in 1979 was awarded an honorary doctorate at the Royal Institute of Technology in Stockholm. In June 1992 the government awarded Anders Franzén the title of Professor. He died in 1993.

In 1628, Sweden had begun her march towards her position as a great power, and by 1658, the kingdom had reached its furthest extent.

1626: ... 136 ...
... 34 ... 40000:
1627: ... Gustavus ... 14000:
1628: ... 40000:
1629: ... Gustavus ... 14000:
108000:

On December 23rd, 1624, it was agreed to build four ships at Stockholm shipyard at the end of the 1620's. One of the larger ships named here was the Vasa.

1626: a large ship of 136 feet between stems and width – 34 feet on deck	40,000:
1627: a small ship as large as the *Gustavus*	14,000:
1628: a large	40,000:
1629: a ship like the *Gustavus*	14,000:
	108,000:

THE DISASTER

SWEDEN always has been and still is to a great extent dependent on sea transport. In the seventeenth century, just as today, the sea also became an invaluable moat.

By the early summer of 1628, the great commander of the Habsburg Empire, Wallenstein, and his troops were at the Baltic. Somewhat in advance, the Emperor had already appointed him »Admiral of the Baltic and the Oceanic Seas«. After Stralsund, Wallenstein had already captured Wismar and other Baltic ports, in order to lay the foundations from there for fleets which were to make him the lord of the sea, and he was already casting covetous looks at Öresund. With this »Key to the Baltic« in his possession, he would be able to control all trade and shipping at all the Baltic ports. That was a serious threat to Sweden.

Hitherto, however, the Emperor had had no fleet in the Baltic. But he had decided to send the Spanish fleet to reinforce the squadrons Wallenstein was forming in Wismar. If the Spaniards came up into our fairway, the situation would become precarious. Stralsund was for the moment the most important goal for Wallensteins plans. The main base of the Imperial fleet was to be there. The old Hansa town heroically defended itself against Wallenstein's attack and finally turned to the two Nordic kings with requests for help. Rapid assistance was dispatched from both the Danes and the Swedes. Three months later, Wallenstein was forced to withdraw his troops after suffering great losses. This was his first adversity of the war and a serious blow to his plans for the Baltic. King Gustaf II Adolf had by now also entered into an important alliance with Stralsund, giving him a firm footing on German soil.

But alarm clouds were gathering over the Baltic Sea skies. Gutav Adolf needed naval warfare forces to fulfill his plans. Impatiently, he urged his advisers to hasten the expansion of the fleet, in which the Vasa was an important link.

In the spring of 1628, the Swedish naval fleet's latest addition, *Ny Wassan* (New Vasa) – the Vasa's original name – was already at the old shipyard by the Tre Kronor (Three Crowns) Palace. The ship was moored next to what was called the gun-crane, the crew working to the full taking on board and stowing the the ballast.

In July, she was again below the gun-crane, this time to take on board her guns and ammunition. The entire artillery store at the time was attached to the palace. In the meantime the Vasa had probably been towed over to the naval establishment in Old Skeppsholmen for diverse works on her. Once the ballast had been taken on board, there almost certainly remained various work to be carried out before the ship could be considered ready for the coming expedition to sea. By July 31st the work was finished and the day of departure was rapidly approaching. There must have been a great deal of talk about the king's new ship in the capital. Even measured by international standards the Vasa was a great ship.

Between three and four in the afternoon of Sunday August 10th, Captain Söfring Hansson gave the order to cast off. Slowly, the Vasa was towed out from her place by the crane. Her maiden voyage had begun. In calm and lovely weather, with a light south-west wind the Vasa was towed along Skeppsbron. The great lion figurehead, glowing in its colours, gazed grimly over towards the slopes of South Stockholm. Men were all ready at the handspikes round the great capstan to start their circular march to wind up the huge anchor hawser. The march began and as the anchor hawser curled in, the Vasa moved slowly forward. In one of the ship's boats, a new anchor was already being rowed in for the next round. The road from the palace down to the water outside the heights of Söder is long considering the anchors, manpower and capstan.

There were many people out and about in town, vespers were just over and the churches emptying. A large number of Stockholm's roughly 10,000 people had come out to enjoy this late summer evening and to witness the ship's departure. On board was Chief Ordnance Master Erik Jönsson, the commander of the naval force in which the Vasa was to be included. As emergency squadron, this force was at first to be stationed at the naval base of Älvsnabben in the Stockholm archipelago and, apart from the Vasa, comprised the two large ships the *Stora Kronan* [Great Crown] and the *Gamla Svärdet* [The Old Sword]. Among the officers on board the Vasa were also Lieutenant Petter Gierdsson, Shipmaster Joen Matsson, Master

View of Stockholm by W. Hartman dated 1650.
The shipyard had by then been moved to the present Skeppsholmen.

Stockholm shipyard as it may have looked in the 1620's
with the Vasa on the slipway. The Three Crowns palace in the background.
Model in the Vasa Museum.

Gunner Joen Larsson and Chief Boatswain Per Bertilsson. The old Captain Hans Jonsson was also on board. He had been a ship's captain as long ago as at the end of the previous century and after that during the course of the years also in charge of the shipyard at Skeppsholmen. Some lucky civilians – wives and children of those on board – had been given permission to go on board for part of the way. In the regulations for service on board the following is included: »Should any man wish to have his wife with him, he is free to do so here in Strömmen or out in the archipelago but not on any voyage involving action against the enemy.« Everything on board was secured and made ready to go to sea. All gun tackle was secured and belayed – only one small one pounder, called *falkon*, lying on deck and with no gun-carriage, was not secured.

So preparations were now made to set sail. To make manoeuvering easier, Captain Söfring had a cable taken to the shore from the stern in order to make it easier and quicker to get the bows to bear eastwards in the direction of the course. Work on the anchor was swiftly completed and from the shore, men could be seen climbing up to free the sails. The deck crew were ready at braces, sheets and halyards. Resembling huge blinds, the topsails were stretched on the fore- and main masts, and the foresail and mizzen fixed.

The stern cable was cast off, the wind not strong, the south cliffs providing lee. With only four sails hoisted, the ship was moving quite slowly with scarcely any steerage-way. Then the wind increased slightly. Water began to swirling round the bows and rippling faintly round the sturdy oak hull. The Vasa fired »*svensk lösen*« *(two shots)*.

A fierce gust from the clifftops made the ship heel over, but then she straightened up again. Slowly, the Vasa slipped along the southern shores, the evening sun high above the lake Mälaren, its rays giving lustre to the colours and gold of the richly decorated stern, the cliffs still providing lee. The small boats that had set out on to the waters of Strömmen on this lovely Sunday evening were easily able to keep up in the wash of the great ship, the people on them waving a last farewell to the Vasa and her crew.

Beyond what was then the bay at Tegelviken, the wind was suddenly given much freer play and again a gust of wind from inland made the Vasa unexpectedly heel fiercely over. All at once, she straightened up again, but this fierce careening had caused some uneasiness. The captain shouted through his megaphone that all men should immediately go to their stations, and he gave orders to loosen the topsail sheets. But the wind was not even strong enough to pull the new rope through the well-greased blocks and help was actually needed to ease them through.

On August 10th, 1628, the disaster occurs. The Vasa capsizes and sinks just as her maiden voyage was about to begin. Drawing by Nils Stödberg.

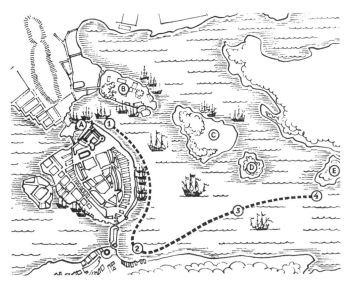

1. From the Three Crowns palace, the Vasa was warped against the south-westerly wind to 2. outside Tranbodarna, where the sails were set. At 3. she began to list and 4. marks the disaster spot.
A. The oldest shipyard established by Gustav Vasa.
B. Towards the end of the sixteenth century, the naval shipyard was moved to Käpplingholmen, called Skeppsholmen for a while, now Blasieholmen.
C. Lustholmen, previously Vangsholmen. The shipyard was moved here according to a decision made in 1630, the present Skeppsholmen.
D. Kastellholmen.
E. Beckholmen.

She heeled over again. The list was even greater this time, and water began rushing in through the open gun-ports. The list increased even further until the Vasa's railing was in the water. Her moment of destiny had come. Just off Beckholmen, she went to the bottom »at full sail, flags and all«.

Were Stockholmers really able to grasp what a catastrophe it was that had occurred? Was it possible that an accident of this kind could happen to the king's most handsome ship, in front of the very eyes of the inhabitants of the capital? The Vasa had just been sailing as proudly as a swan out towards the archipelago and suddenly she no longer existed. Loose objects and hatches were floating around and people were swimming for their lives and crying out in mortal anguish. A great many boats swiftly arrived at the spot and everything was done to save whatever could be saved.

No one knows with any certainty how many people were on board. According to available crew recommendations, however, the crew on the Vasa should have consisted of 133 seamen. The intention had been that 300 soldiers as well were to be on board, but fortunately they had not yet embarked. On the other hand, those on board included women and children. No one knows how many died. It is said that old Captain Hans Jonsson was drowned and that Ordnance Master Erik Jönsson and the captain »got away after being for a long time under the water in great danger of their lives«. No list has ever been found in any of the archives of those who were saved or those who died.

At the most, fifty or so people probably died in the disaster. In the excavation after the salvaging, however, only skeletons and parts of skeletons of twenty-five people were found.

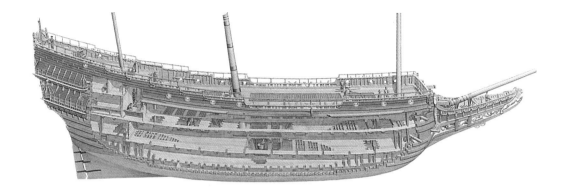

**The various decks can be seen in this drawing of the Vasa.
Farthest down in the hold is a deck of loosely laid planks. Then follows
the orlop deck, the lower gun-deck, the upper gun-deck and the upper deck.
The capstans on the upper deck and the lower gun-deck can also be seen,
as well as the galley midships in the hold.**
Drawing by Julian Osbaldstone.

**Admiral Baron Carl Carlsson Gyllenheim (1574–1650),
halfbrother of King Gustav II Adolf. Private collection.**

Claes Larsson Fleming (1592–1644) was Vice-Admiral from 1620.

THE TRIAL

THE INEXPLICABLE fate of the Vasa caused a huge stir and great grief among high and low in the capital, then gradually all over the country. A serious mistake must have been made, otherwise a ship simply could not have been lost in the way the Vasa had. Long after, the terrible disaster must have been the all-overshadowing subject of talk not only in the streets and market squares, inns and beer joints, but also in people's homes. Survivors of the unlucky ship must have more than once been offered a beer and a tot of spirits to relate their experiences to their inquisitive fellow-men. At the time, more or less truthful testimonies, stories, rumours and gossip were the main sources of news.

Preliminary hearings by state councillors on the accident began at Stockholm Palace the very next day, to which the captain, who had only just escaped with his life, and the »Master Shipbuilder of Holmen« were both summoned. Captain Söfring had been taken into custody at the palace as soon as he had come ashore, but was released on bail a few days later.

On September 5th, a major enquiry was held at the palace by an especially arranged court consisting of seventeen people, of which six were state councillors. The Admiral of the Fleet, Carl Carlsson Gyllenhielm, acted as chairman.

Before he died in 1984, Commander-Captain Georg Hafström, the maritime historian, managed to carry out a major work which spread light on the Vasa accident. Among other things, it was thanks to his researches and publications, that from quite early on what had preceded was evident in this dismal context.

The records of this major enquiry are preserved only in a fragmentary copy, but they nevertheless provide certain opportunities to assess the causes of the accident and a reconstruction of the trial. The techniques of the hearing do not appear to have been particularly advanced. The intention to try to find a scapegoat quickly is very clear. Not least with the knowledge of the severe punishments of the day, it is impossible not to feel pity for those involved in the drama. It is also understandable that the atmosphere must occasionally have been ominously tense.

The first to be put up against the wall was the man appointed by King Gustav II Adolf to lead the naval force, Chief Ordnance Master Erik Jönsson, who would probably not have had any direct function when it came to the running and man-oeuvering of the ship. As an artillerist, he had been primarily interested in the Vasa's guns. He also stated that he had already inspected the guns before the Vasa had heeled over the first time, i.e. before the setting of the sails, while the ship was still lying at Tranbodarna. He had found nothing wrong, and all the guns had been secured. When the vessel began heeling over, Erik Jönsson ran back to the gun-deck. The water had already begun to pour in through the gun-ports. He had shou-ted for them to loosen the sheets, but that had already been done. The water rose swiftly, so far up in the interior of the ship that the stairs down to the battery deck floated away. At the very last moment, Erik Jönsson managed to save himself up on to the deck.

During the hearing, Erik Jönsson showed no great faith in the Vasa. Among other things, he stated that in his opinion, the Vasa would have capsized even if she had not been under sail. The superstructure was far too high, he considered, and the ship »was heavier above than below«. The Admiral pointed out that Jönsson was nevertheless appointed to the Vasa as Vice-Admiral, so he should also have found out whether the ship was correctly ballasted. To this, Erik Jönsson said that he was neither a Captain nor a Vice-Admiral, nor had he ever made himself out to be any such thing. He was the chief ordnance master, so considered the captain and the skipper understood more about ballast than he did.

The Admiral of the Fleet stated in conclusion that if the shipmaster had known the ship was unstable and therefore been instructed, he would have had her ballas-ted down yet another foot. Erik Jönsson's reply to that statement was short but elo-quent. How could he have done that, when the gun-ports were no more than three and a half foot above water level with the ballast they already had.

Then it was the turn of Lieutenant Petter Gierdsson, who had been in charge of the rigging of the Vasa. He had also been ordered on board during the vessel's brief maiden voyage. He was immediately accused of not informing anyone that the ship was abnormally unstable – a circumstance the lieutenant maintained he did not know about. He had been concerned only with the rigging and he had not even seen

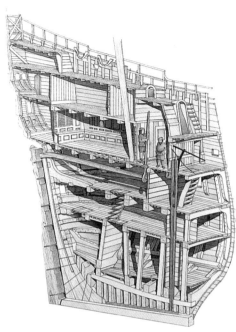

The officers lived in the sterncastle, astern of the mizzen mast. Aft of the steerage was the main cabin, above it a slightly smaller cabin and above that, further astern, was the poop-royal cabin. Drawing by Daniel Isaksson.

To the fore of the great cabin was the steerage where the helmsman handled the whipstaff. This runs through a roller bearing to the deck below, where it is connected to the tiller, which in its turn is fastened to the rudder. To the fore of the steerage is a pump made of a bored-out alder trunk. Drawing by Susanne Edlund.

One of the accusations taken to the court was that the guns were said not to have been lashed and so had started to roll and caused the disaster. This was denied, which could be confirmed at the salvaging. All the gun-carriages were in place in their gun-ports and in many places the lashings remained.

what kind of ballast had been taken on board. Gierdsson also stated that all the guns were well secured. The gun-ports were about four and a half foot from the water and the ship's draught was fourteen and a half foot to the fore and sixteen astern, and »15 shoes in the hold«. He also stated that he had never believed that any ship could capsize in such a light wind. Lieutenant Gierdsson had no opinion on why the Vasa heeled over so easily – whether she was badly built or had too little ballast. With almost more than permissable modesty, he stated that he knew nothing about it, for he did not understand shipbuilding, and nor had he seen what kind or how much ballast the ship was carrying.

The next man was Shipmaster Jöran Matsson. He must have been a very special man. The accusation against him was extremely serious. In the records it says as follows: »that he had presumably not understood his vocation or Office and that he had not attended to both ballast and other matters as his vocation and Office required and demanded, so that H.M. ship had come to misfortune.«

To this accusation, the shipmaster replied that he had stowed in as much ballast as the hold could contain. He also personally supervised the men's work by going down into the hold himself with candles to level and stow in as much as he could. Jöran Matsson also considered he had done his best to fulfil his duties.

The enquiry was approaching its climax when Shipmaster Matsson was asked whether before the accident he had noticed that the ship was unstable. The shipmaster then produced a sensational revelation. Captain Söfring had told Admiral Fleming that the ship was unstable. When the Vasa was lying by the gun-crane below the palace with her ballast on board, Matsson went on, they had tested it out. While the Admiral was on board, they had ordered thirty men to run from one side of the ship to the other. The first time, she heeled over the width of a plank, the second time two, the third time three plank widths. Then the Admiral requested that the test should be stopped; »had they run any more times, she would have capsized completely«, said »The Fleming«. And when this happened, he said he wished that H.M. was at home. On this occasion all the ballast had been loaded except one small boatload.

However, Shipmaster Matsson stated that if it was the will of God that the ship be salvaged and loaded down over the gun-ports, »then she will capsize anyhow. The Vasa is far too narrow at the bottom and lacks belly. I had already told Admiral Fleming this when we took on the ballast,« maintained the pugnacious shipmaster. Fleming had replied, Matsson went on, »you have too much ballast, the gun-ports will be too close to the water«. »God willing, that she will stand upright on her keel«, Matsson is said to have replied, to which the Admiral retorted: »The master shipbuilder surely has built ships before, so Matsson need have no worries of that kind.«

It can be imagined what a stir this testimony must have caused in the session hall, with all this inflammatory material the good shipmaster was serving up.

Then finally Matsson stated that all the guns had been well secured. He also said that if the ship could not tolerate the small sails in the prevailing calm weather at the time of the accident, how would she then manage the topgallant sail and all the other sails in truly windy weather.

They were all clearly slipping out of the court's grasp. But someone must nevertheless be guilty. So they latched on to the unfortunate Chief Boatswain Per Bertilsson. He was asked why he had not seen to the sails, ropes and guns properly. At the same time, he was asked whether he had not perchance also been drunk. The poor man plucked up his courage and replied: »That day I was attending Holy Communion of our Lord.« And there they were, again, without having found anyone who had failed in his duty.

Now it was the turn of Master Shipbuilder Hein Jacobsson to take the stand in court. He was asked why he had built the Vasa ship so narrow, so badly and without belly, so that it had capsized.

The question was easy for the master shipbuilder to answer and almost turned into a boomerang. The ship was built, said Hein Jacobsson, according to the »serte« [contract to build a ship according to certain measurements] provided by Master Henrik [Hybertsson, died in 1627] and on the orders of the king. The ship is even one foot and five thumbs wider than on the original plans. Nor was the master shipbuilder slow in maintaining that everyone considered the ship well built.

Arendt Hybertsson de Groot, Master Henrik's brother and a merchant, was asked for the reason why the ship had been given such large superstructures. Nor did de Groot seem to be particularly scared or impressed by these accusations. He must also have felt safe in this context simply to be able to refer to the the king's own elevated decision. Arendt de Groot answered as precisely as Master Shipbuilder Hein Jacobsson had, that the ship was built according to the *serte* he had contracted with the king and in agreement with the prototype he had shown His Royal Majesty. This was of a French vessel, built in Holland for the Duke de Guise. There is nothing wrong with the ship's construction, de Groot continued his argument, except that it should have been properly ballasted.

But the master shipbuilder had on some occasion said to Captain Söfring, the prosecutor stated, that this ship was as stiff as St Per's and should even be able to sail without any ballast. However, Master Shipbuilder Jacobsson did not admit to

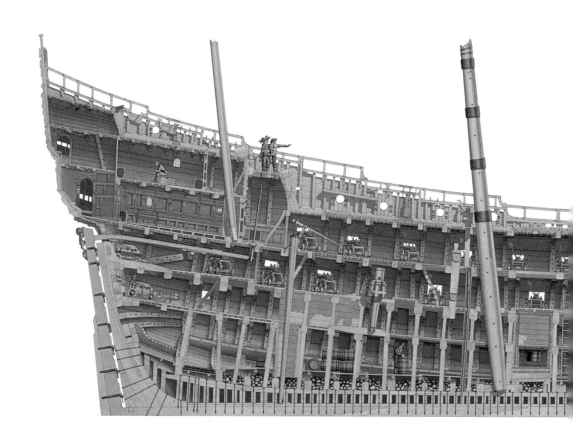

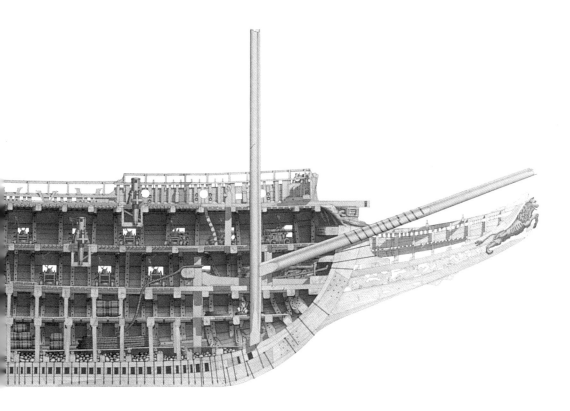

**The find of the Vasa has meant an invaluable source of knowledge of
how a large warship in the early 1600's was constructed.**
Drawing by Robert Stone.

TECHNICAL DATA:

Total length (including bowsprit)	69.0 m
Greatest width	11.7 m
Draught	4.8 m
Total height – at main mast	52.5 m
Height of sternship	19.3 m
Displacement	1 210 tons
Area of sail	1 275 sqm
Number of sails	10

Guns: 64 guns, of which 48 24-pounders,
eight 3-pounders, two 1-pounders and
six mortars.

Crew	145 men
	300 soldiers

any such statement. On the contrary, he maintained, that with more ballast inside, the ship would not have capsized.

In brief, in the slightly acid exchange of words that now followed, Captain Söfring replied in much the same manner as the chief ordnance master had. If the Vasa had had more ballast inside, then the scuppers would have come below the water level. The gun-ports would have come so close to the water that the guns would have been useless. In the same way, he went on, there was a danger of the same thing happening to a ship now almost completed, a ship being built in the same way as the Vasa. The master shipbuilder replied to this that he had to build it according to the *serte* he had been given. To both these remarks, the prosecutor quite diplomatically replied that he would also question other sensible men on the matter.

If all master shipbuilders are allowed to look at the ship, said Arendt de Groot, they will all say the ship is built so that it is »*faultless*« . If the ship is »*faultlessly*« built, the prosecutor asked, why then did it capsize? That question was referred to higher powers, »they knew nothing, only God knows« The king has been told by me, said Arendt de Groot, how long and wide the ship was and he was satisfied with that information and wanted it to be so.

The prosecutor was clearly not satisfied with the answers he had received from the shipbuilders. He made various attempts to get at Messrs Jacobsson and de Groot with insidious questions. For a long time the hearing circled round this extremely touchy and essential problem. If the king wanted the ship designed according to the contract, then those who had been entrusted with the building ought to have informed the king what was correct, the prosecutor said, among other things. Did the shipbuilder otherwise consider that it was compatible with good sense and conscience to build a ship such as the Vasa?

But clearly it was not possible to lure the shipbuilder away from the answer formula. He replied: It is as well built as any ship can be. Another tricky jab from the prosecutor: naturally the ship is well built, but it is not of the correct proportions.

The prosecutor again returns to the main question. This time he turns directly to de Groot. As the contract is between the king and you, then you ought to have consulted with the shipbuilder to ensure the ship was properly built, in other words so that the king could make use of it. Again the reply came according to the old formula – as de Groot had commissioned the ship with the king, so had the building of it been carried out as well as it could be. With that the discussion on the construction and building of the Vasa was clearly over as far as the shipbuilders were concerned.

Finally, a man by the name of Johan Isbrandsson was then summoned. Why had he, a servant of the king, not better controlled the building of the ship so that it had been better built and able to withstand both seas and wind? Why had he not protested that the part of the ship above the water was heavier than the part below the waterline?

To this Isbrandsson replied that as far as he understood the art of shipbuilding, he had not been able to find any faults, and he considered the Vasa to be correctly built and with all sails set should be able to go to sea. Isbrandsson also maintained that the Vasa was as wide as the *Kronan*. He judged her a good ship, even better than the *Kronan*.

Again the question was asked: Why did the Vasa capsize? Well, Isbrandsson did not know that either. It seemed to him to be totally impossible that a ship of that kind could topple over. Then Isbrandsson was finally asked how high above the waterline the gun-ports were on the *Kronan*. About four foot, was the answer. Captain Frans was dispatched to measure. And he is still on his way.

The salvaging of the Vasa was carried out with conventional methods.
The principle had long been clear but it had not been possible
to put it into practice. Olaus Magnus describes the procedure in 1555
like this in *Historia de gentibus septentrionalibus*.

ABSENT VERDICT

FOR a fateful period, Sweden, seen from both a military-political and national-economic viewpoint, had been afflicted by extremely tangible losses. In 1615, the Council had already found cause to complain about »that the fleet, on which the realm's welfare depends, in earlier times of war, is very run-down and much reduced«. Since 1620, with considerable intensity, attempts had been made to build up the fleet, but owing to losses at war, fires and losses in storms at sea, it had been severely depleted. So it is understandable that the leaders of the nation must have looked on the loss of the Vasa with great seriousness.

Financially, the disaster certainly meant a great many things. A warship the size of the Vasa cost about 40,000 riksdaler, money laboriously earned by the taxpayers and now to no purpose quite literally thrown into the sea. State funds were often low, so it was quite understandable that Captain Söfring Hansson had been arrested the moment he came ashore. The keenness to arrange a hearing and trial very quickly to find and punish the sinner was also understandable. Even more strange is that nothing ever came of the case.

Naturally the reason for this may give rise to speculations. None of the names of those sitting in judgement are known for certain. But there is reason to suppose that the state counsellors Johan Skytte, Klas Horn, the brother of the chancellor Gabriel Gustafsson Oxenstierna, Per Brahe the Younger and Karl Oxenstierna were among others there. It is also known that Captain, later Vice-Admiral Hans Clerck, Captain, later Lieutenant-Admiral Lars Bubb (ennobled Rosenskiöld), Hans Foratt and the well-known ironmaster, Willem de Besche at Finspång participated. Also present were the Treasurer, Erik Larsson (later ennobled von der

Linde) and the Mayor of Stockholm, Hans Nilsson.

The court's chairman, Admiral Carl Carlsson Gyllenhielm – half brother to King Gustav II Adolf – was not exactly a fledgling. He had among other things participated as field commander in his father's King Karl IX's campaign in Livland, where he had shown both courage and skill. For twelve years he had been imprisoned by the Poles, six of them in chains. This long imprisonment had quite naturally robbed the Admiral of a great deal of his physical and spiritual vigour. But he was no broken man. For nearly ten years, from 1619 onwards, he had been the Navy's senior officer, and on several occasions had successfully been in charge of its destiny at sea.

It does really appear incredible that these gentlemen had been unable to succeed in finding out the real cause of the accident. The ship's real builder, Master Henrik Hybertsson, had indeed died in 1627, so could not be brought to court. But they nevertheless had two responsible men to feel the pulse when it came to the construction and building of the vessel, namely Master Shipbuilder Hein Jacobsson and Master Henrik's brother, Arent de Groot.

Could it possibly be that Shipmaster Matsson's sensational testimony had saved those involved from judgement and punishment? In that case, he had done a considerable service to his fellow-men in misfortune. For punishments at the time were severe. If anyone had been considered guilty, they would certainly have had to forfeit their lives for their neglect. According to the maritime articles of 1644, for instance, if a first mate ran a ship aground as a result of careless navigation, he would be keelhauled and had to pay for damage done. Anyone carelessly causing a fire on board would be thrown into the same fire.

But, as mentioned before, no one was found guilty, anyhow, nowhere can it be read that anyone was sentenced. Shipmaster Matsson had undeniably put the court members in an unpleasant situation. After all, he had almost made Admiral Fleming, the nearest man to the Admiral of the Fleet, to appear to have neglected his duty. The master shipbuilder had also succeeded in washing his hands of it all by persistently blaming the king. As the latter himself had approved and confirmed the calculations used, it was difficult for the court to determine directly that the calculations had been faulty. As long as the Vasa remained on the bottom of Strömmen, there was no possibility of finding evidence that she had been faultily built.

Had Admiral Fleming held back his opinions on the stability of the Vasa only from some kind of misdirected consideration for his lord and king? Had he never believed in the stability test, or had he just hoped that all would eventually be all right?

It will probably never be known why the experienced Fleming played down the extremely important test that clearly showed that the Vasa was unstable. Admiral Fleming's statement as found in the records of the hearing after Shipmaster Matsson's testimony, is undeniably quite contradictory. At first the Admiral requests that the stability test be stopped, for »had they run any more times she would have capsized«. He also pronounced a wish that the king himself had been there. Somewhat later, he tells Matsson not to worry about the ship's stability as the master shipbuilder had built ships before! As far as is known, Fleming never publicly denied or verified this troublesome testimony, something that must be considered highly peculiar.

However, the Vasa investigation did have certain repercussions. In Sweden at the time, there were several foreigners contracted to maintain and fit older ships and to build new ships for the Navy. Among these entrepeneurs can be named the two brothers from Scotland, Richard and Hans Clerck, later admirals in the service of the Swedish Navy. They maintained the tackle on all the ships of the fleet in Stockholm from 1615 until 1628. In Stockholm, several ships were built by the aforementioned Master Shipbuilder Henrik Hybertsson, and in Göteborg by Albrekt von Velden. In this context, Master Shipbuilders Paridon von Horn and Kristian Wilshusen from Holland should also be mentioned, as well as Anton Monier from Brussels.

The entrepeneur and leasing system relieved the Admiralty of various detailed duties, but it did have major drawbacks. It turned out that quite soon several of the contractors had begun to neglect their assignments. Even before the disaster, Admiral Fleming had several times found cause to criticize carelessness, including with the ships' equipment. The ship's captains had also openly informed the Admiral of their discontent with the system. King Gustav Adolf had even threatened the contractor gentlemen with his disfavour. In 1628, he sure enough lost patience and wrote to Fleming, who was with the fleet off Danzig, that he should make his way home and ensure that »Skeppsholmen and all concerning the activities there carried out in a fitting manner«. After his homecoming, Fleming also arranged for a hard-handed raid on the entrepeneurs. The entire contract system was abandoned and one or two of the most comprehensive contracts – the tackle leasing and shipyard leasing – were cancelled at the end of 1628. From 1629 onwards, the Crown itself took over the maintenance of the ships, anyhow partly, though ships continued to be built on contract. It is probably more than likely that the Vasa's ignominious maiden voyage contributed to the demise of the contracting system.

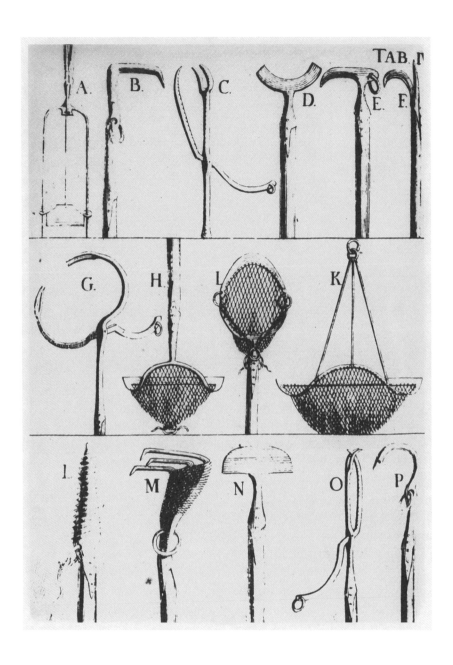

Divers in the seventeenth century had many specially constructed tools
available for cutting away, breaking up, holding firm,
collecting and picking things up from the depths below.
Examples of tools of this kind have here been taken from
Mårten Triewald's book *The Art of living under Water*, Stockholm 1743.

PIONEERS IN THE DEPTHS

THE MESSAGE of the Vasa disaster was soon borne on the sustaining wings of rumour far beyond the borders of Sweden. It is easy to understand that reliable inventors, treasure-seekers and intriguing adventurers were soon sniffing the air for easily caught prey when they heard about a new, well-equipped warship sinking almost right inside the sheltered harbour of the Swedish capital, including sixty-four good guns and the hope of a well-filled cash chest on board. For nearly sixty years – to be more specific, from August 13th 1628 right up until August 1683 – the battle over the Vasa continued with more or less undiminished intensity. Sometimes duels of words went on before the Public Notary or Svea Court of Appeal, where cases might be concerned with fraud and treachery between intimate friends. Sometimes more or less fruitless efforts were made to rob the Vasa of articles of value she had hidden down there, thirty-two metres below sea-level. Thirty-two metres, that ridiculously close lay the Vasa, and yet her desirable treasures were so distant, so difficult to reach.

The men trying their luck in salvage operations were a colourful lot. Many nationalities were represented among the treasure-seekers. The list of them seeking the favours of the Council begins with an Englishman, then come a French captain, a Dutch master shipbuilder, a Swede, a Lübeckian, a Mr. Carl Carlsson of unknown nationality, a Scottish baron, another Scot, a mechanic from Riga, a Swedish war commissioner, another Englishman, and many more. Intrigues galore occurred to acquire the Council's licence to salvage sunken ships for the Crown, the Vasa always to the fore in their minds. Words were seldom muted when it came to describing the skills they had at saving even large ships from Ran the god of the sea. In the name of justice, it should also be said that some of these gentlemen really did carry out truly great deeds in their trade. Their technical resources were poor, their equipment extremely primitive, and yet they did not back away from these major tasks.

The Englishman, Ian Bulmer – the first man to dare a salvage attempt according to the regulations – started work three days after the disaster. According to contemporary records, in quite a short time he succeeded in righting the Vasa. Whether this is true, and in that case how he carried it out, nothing is known today, but anyhow, the Vasa was standing on her keel when she was again found by Anders Franzén.

The mind reels when one reads about people in the seventeenth century seriously attempting to raise the Vasa. Ships and boats were situated above the wreck and their »instruments« were trimmed. These were grappling irons and anchors, with which they tried to hook on to gun-ports and other suitable places. Then they tried to fasten the cables to the capstan and wind in. But the weight was too great and their attempts were doomed to failure.

However, the king was extremely keen to bring the Vasa up as soon as possible. Bulmer was clearly not working fast enough. As soon as Willem de Besche had arrived in Stockholm, he had to tackle the difficult assignment of heading the salvage operation. As a collaborator he had the ex-shipmaster of the Vasa, Captain Söfring Hansson. But the Vasa defied all efforts. Not even when Admiral Fleming himself took over supervision in the autumn did they manage to bring her up. In the end it was judged that all efforts would be in vain without the help of divers. In that case divers had to be recruited from Holland, Fleming points out in a letter to King Gustav II Adolf in November 1628. However, it was not Holland they turned to at first. Instead, Governor Henrik Månsson of Kexholm castle in Karelia, Finland, was ordered to look for divers. He was given authority to tell them that they would be working on salvaging the Vasa and to promise them good pay.

In July 1629, Admiral Fleming again wrote to King Gustav II Adolf: »As far as the Vasa is concerned, they have been working with great industry on bringing her up, though hitherto little has been achieved, the reason for this partly that the barges with the *Gamla Svärdet* are not strong enough to bear the weight that is down below, and partly the blocks and chains break when the work is at its busiest, so again the work is delayed so long while everything is repaired and fixed. I have now had *Nya Svärdet* brought there to help the others and had the blocks furnished with iron. Have also again fastened 17 strong hawsers and chains, with which we will now this week, weather permitting, try all that is possible to achieve. The weight is greater than I have at any time could have presumed.« But nor was it successful this time. Clearly all was as if bewitched, the difficulties unsurmountable, and as far as can be judged, the authorities gave up any further salvage attempts on their part.

But there were many people wanting to try their luck. Salvage experts relieved one another at regular intervals, avidly guarding their working methods, and the Council was obliged not to reveal anything about them, nor to use the methods themselves without the consent of whomever it concerned.

For about ten years, salvage attempts on the Vasa continued unabated. Then followed a somewhat eventless decade from the salvaging point of view. But just after 1650, however, the Vasa again came into focus. The Scottish baron, an ex-colonel in the Swedish Army, Alexander Forbes, declared himself willing to try to salvage both the Vasa and other sunken ships. The colonel had quite recently lost all his possessions in a shipwreck, so his own interest in diving and salvaging had been aroused. As he had been of great service to the Swedes, he also succeeded in procuring from Queen Kristina the sole right for twelve years to carry out at his own expense salvaging activities in Swedish waters. Forbes was not an expert in the field himself, but he was given permission to acquire knowledgeable assistants from elsewhere. During the first years of his licence, Forbes had three companions, among them Ian Bulmer, but before his assistants had had time to carry out a single salvage operation, all three of them had died.

Forbes now tried to make his licence profitable in another way, by contracting out the salvaging of the Vasa and the Danish flagship *Sophia* to a consortium, the members of which included the Scottish diver, Jacob Maule, and a Swedish colonel by the name of Hans Albrecht von Treileben.

As far as can be judged, von Treileben was a dangerous man to work with. In a fairly short time, he succeeded in manoeuvering Forbes out before his licence had run out. In 1658, he was able to take over the desirable salvage licence, which gave him the right to carry on his activities for the following twenty-one years, together with at the most twenty assistants. However, he was not allowed to touch the Vasa. In order for Treileben to acquire the required material and be able to make a living, he was also given the right to bring in and take out certain duty-free goods during the licence period – certainly no poor advantage. On paper, this was valued at 2,400 silver riksdaler per year. It is perhaps not entirely wrong to presume that, skilfully exploited, this advantage could provide considerably more than that sum.

Treileben now held all the trumps in his hand. He had not only acquired the main part of Forbes' licence – he had also robbed his ex-employer of his technical expertise. Treileben's working party included the diving specialist, Maule. The colonel was obviously a clever organiser and an energetic pusher. The work was immediately begun and quite soon Treileben was able to note considerable progress.

In 1663, a new salvage expert appears on the scene – Andreas Peckell. He has learnt quite a lot about diving in Lübeck and has a special interest in the Vasa's valuable guns. Behind Treileben's back, Peckell gradually tries to start co-operating with Maule. The game of intrigue is again in action. Testimony of this comes not least from the trial records preserved for posterity. The Vasa was still the property of Forbes, but Treileben had probably had some idea of trying to make capital out of the old wreck by working together with Forbes. This failed, and instead he established a probably rather profitable co-operation with Peckell. Treileben finally manoeuvered Forbes out and appropriated the Vasa on behalf of himself and his assistants.

The ship had now lain down there on the bottom for thirty-five years, and nor had the wreck fared all that well. Grappling irons and anchors had lacerated her sides and superstructure. Hawsers, remains of rigging, old cables, chains and all kinds of dross cluttered the deck. So the first task Peckell and his workmen had was to clear it all away, though the idea of seeing the Vasa once again afloat had not been dropped. But Peckell and Treileben were primarily merchants in the salvaging business and wanted quick returns for their efforts. This meant bringing up as much of value as possible in the shortest possible time.

These two go-ahead friends had undertaken a gigantic enterprise, and spirit and initiative also marked their contribution. Peckell and his workmen must have toiled like beasts of burden. An Italian priest and explorer, Francesco Negri, has provided a detailed eye-witness account of this activity out in Strömmen almost three hundred and fifty years ago. Thanks to this account, which was printed in 1700, it is possible today to acquire a good grasp of the tools and working methods used by these pioneers in the field of the art of diving and salvaging.

Francesco Negri describes the activities like this – One lovely autumn day at the end of October in 1663, we set off out on to Strömmen. A light breeze is blowing and we are sailing fairly swiftly down towards the place where the Vasa ship capsized and sank many years ago. A small boat has been at anchor there for some time, a clumsy craft, rather dirty and also somewhat worse for the wear, several larger and smaller working boats lying round her. Intense salvage attempts are being made here under the leadership of the Treileben-Peckell consortium. The boat deck is cluttered with all kinds of mysterious equipment, large cables, blocks and hoisting hawsers – sturdy gear intended for lifting heavy articles. They are primarily aiming to attempt to bring up the Vasa's valuable bronze guns. These weigh up to a ton each and it is clear that sturdy equipment is required to manage such weights. The work is led by the experienced Andreas Peckell, who considers it impossible at the moment to raise the Vasa. So first of all the great ship has to be relieved of all her guns and then attempts made to remove her ballast. After that, Peckell optimistically thinks, it should be fairly simple to raise the ship to the surface again. To raise the pieces placed on the two gundecks, special tools are intended to tear away part of the planking of the upper deck.

A number of prominent personages have been out recently and studied with interest this epoch-making working method launched by the consortium.

Messrs Peckell and Treileben have a remarkable invention at their disposal – what is called a diving bell, with the help of which a man, at no risk, can go down to great depths and stay there for almost half an hour. With such effective aids, the salvage work should go relatively easily. This new invention had already been successfully tried out on a number of occasions here in Sweden, among them on the west coast. Treileben introduced his fantastic diving equipment as early as in 1658, but this is the first time it has been in use in Stockholm waters. Unfortunately, the water on the east coast is not as clear and clean as outside Göteborg. The diving experts, however, consider they have had such good experience, they can nevertheless dare to try out their appliances here. The equipment has also been successively improved, and among other things, they have now succeeded in providing the divers with effective protection against the cold.

They are just preparing another descent to the wreck. The diver to go down has sat down on a stool and his colleagues are helping to dress him in the heavy equipment, including double hide or leather boots and a sturdy tunic of the same material, held together by sealing iron rings and bindings. The diver finally puts on to his head a cap or hood of ordinary cloth before labouriously rising to go down to the diving bell, which is standing ready on a small raft mooored alongside the boat.

This amazing diving bell does not really look anything much. It is about one and a quarter metres high and shaped roughly like a church bell. The rather heavy piece is manoeuvered by two men with the help of blocks and tackle.

The bell is now hoisted up about a metre. The diver goes in under the bell and gets up on to a small lead platform. This hangs in ropes a half metre long and fastened to the lower edge of the bell. Assistants hand the diver the tools he needs for his difficult task over thirty metres below the water level. The most important tool is a strong wooden stave, roughly two metres long. At the end of the stave is an iron hook with which the diver is able to grasp any object he has discovered. For the work with the heavy guns, there are several different special tools, large tongs and other grappling tools. When it comes to lifting heavy weights from the wreck, the diver takes a coarse rope with him into the bell, the upper part of which is fastened to the raft and the free end can easily be knotted firmly to the object to be lifted. The guns on the second and third decks have to be eased out through the gun-ports. How this is managed, the experts do not wish to say. A thin signalling rope constitutes the diver's only link with his friends on the float. The diver gives the all clear and the bell is pushed out above the water, then slowly and carefully, this remarkable arrangement is lowered into the depths.

In the upper part of the bell, a cushion of compressed air now forms, so the diver stands in the water in his leather-clad protected body but has his neck and head up in the air-filled space above. After about twenty minutes, our diver reappears. As evidence that he really has been down there by the Vasa, he has brought up with him a heavy oak plank with iron fittings on it. It must be cold in the water. The diver is trembling with cold despite his warm clothes and despite the fact that he is used to this risky work. So far the report of Francesco Negri.

Naturally there were many dangers lying in wait for these bold pioneers. The striving to improve their materials also had its perils. An attempt of this kind almost cost Diver Anders his life. Peckell had had a new breathing apparatus made, a long pipe or tube. Diver Anders was lowered into the water wearing his leather suit and was to try to breathe through the long tube. However, he had not gone far when he was almost suffocated, so had to be immediately drawn back up to the surface again. For eight days, Anders was in a very bad way in bed, spitting blood. After all, long snorkel tubes have even in our day caused accidents among young people and children underwater swimming and sport diving.

The divers of those days must have been bold and courageous men, full of rare and persistent energy. With their simple equipment, they carried out major feats. They managed to raise the main part, or over fifty of the Vasa's guns out of the depths. The exact number is unfortunately not known for certain. According to existing customs documents, 53 of the ship's guns were shipped to Lübeck in 1665. Once they had raised so many guns, interest in the Vasa and work on the ship apparently waned. Treileben found other, presumably more profitable hunting grounds.

The warship was allowed to rest in lone majesty for nearly twenty years until yet another man with salvage as his speciality appears. His name is Liberton and he has a »rare invention« to offer. Liberton requests to take over Treileben's licence. This was granted and in 1683 he begins his work. He managed to raise one of the Vasa's remaining large 24-pounder guns. Liberton offers the piece for sale to the Swedish authorities, but they decline. Their laconic reply was that »the piece he has retrieved from the Vasa he must sell to whomever he can best be bothered.«

The salvagers' boats withdraw. The Vasa is increasingly concealed by silt and dirt from the growing capital. Fish swim undisturbed back and forth inside the dim interior. The long sleep of the Sleeping Beauty has begun. Seafarers of later times were simply annoyed by this mysterious object in the depths that caught hold of their anchors and forced them to cut the anchor hawser to get free.

Fortunately for the historians, it was a collection of colourful troublemakers with a taste for lawsuits who were in the lead of salvaging work in the seventeenth century. Had Forbes and Treileben, Maule and Peckell, at regular intervals not been at each others throats, then perhaps no one would have written down their story. Now the story is well preserved for posterity and thoroughly accounted for in the court annals.

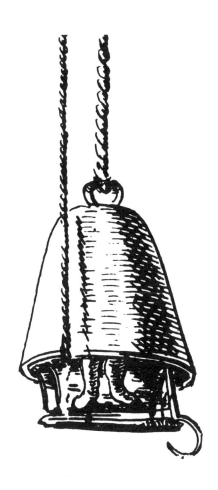

The Vasa as she would have looked with all ten sails set.
Drawing by Nils Stödberg.

THE VASA – A WORLD SENSATION

THE STORY of the Vasa is undeniably unique, entailing little more than a two-hour »sea voyage«, followed by three hundred and thirty years quietly on the seabed. No glorious deeds, no fighting, no battling against severe storms have been noted on her records. She never made any contribution to the defence of Sweden. The milestones in her history are those of foundering and resurrection. She caused dismay and disappointment in her own century, but was greeted in ours with delighted enthusiasm. It is truly a remarkable destiny for a warship – undamaged, to be lost in seveneenth century Sweden, to be woken to life in our day. She has sailed through the centuries with a message to us from the past – an amazing time machine.

The Vasa is in many ways a ship in a class of her own. She is the world's oldest salvaged and fully identified complete ship. She belongs in a period of time in which very little is known of the art of shipbuilding, for in those days drawings in shipbuilding had not begun to be used.

The oldest known corresponding ship is Nelson's famous *Victory*. The keel of this flagship from Trafalgar, however, was laid about 130 years later than that of the Vasa. But there is, or rather have been ships preserved that are older than the Vasa, though the majority have been what are called ceremonial or burial ships, so not intended for ordinary use. Nor are they named or dated as the Vasa is. Caligula's galleys are an example of this. These floating pleasure palaces, which were seventy metres long and twenty metres wide, were probably built by Emperor Caligula (A.D.12–41) and used in Lake Nemi, a crater lake in the Albano mountains just outside Rome. For centuries these galleys caught the imagination of trea-

47

sure-seekers and scholars. Mussolini had both ships salvaged in a very radical manner. Between 1928 and 1931, he had the 167 square kilometre and thirty-four metre deep lake drained. The freed ships were taken up and installed together with other finds in a special museum building by the lake. In the spring of 1944, the Germans burnt down these relics of Roman Antiquity.

In the Norwegian Vikingskipshuset (Viking Ship House) in Bygdöy in Oslo are the restored Gokstad and Oseberg ships, both found on land in huge burial mounds. They are considered to have been built during the ninth and tenth centuries. The Danish Viking ships provided with a museum in Roskilde should also be mentioned here, as well as the Mediaeval German Bremerkoggen, which was given her final resting place in Deutsches Schiffartsmuseum (German Seafaring Museum) in Bremerhaven. In Portsmouth is half of King Henry VIII's flagship the *Mary Rose*. She sank in battle in 1545 and was salvaged in 1981. Since the middle of the 1980's, a great many exciting objects and shipbuilding details from the *Kronan* – another Franzén ship – have been a main attraction at the County Museum in Kalmar in Sweden.

The first sign of life the Vasa gave was a small piece of black oak – the first reward for a lengthy labour of research. The piece of oak set off the alarm to the naval authorities that the lost ship had probably been found. The naval divers were soon able to to establish that the presumption was correct. They went on to find that the warship Vasa had turned into the »ideal wreck« the Vasa. The conditions for salvaging her were described by experts in 1957 as follows:

1. The Vasa was built of oak and the most important units of the hull are probably intact.
2. The Vasa was among other things equipped with 48 corrosion-free bronze 24-pounder guns.
3. The Vasa was a man-of-war which sank fully equipped on her maiden voyage in 1628.
4. The Vasa sank quickly, totally undamaged and with all her equipment on board.
5. The Vasa stands upright on stiff clay.
6. The Vasa is well preserved by conserving layers of sediment.
7. The Vasa has not suffered any damaging effect from ice pressure, the movement of waves, plant or animal life, short-wave light, free oxygen.
8. The Vasa lies close to the capital's naval dockyard, where major resources are available and these can be put into action regardless of weather and wind.

9. The Vasa can be identified with complete certainty.
10. The Vasa is the oldest hitherto found, named and dated ship which is in good state.

In other words, the main combinations surrounding the Vasa have been unusually favourable from the point of view of marine-archaeology and the techniques of salvaging.

The find gave rise to tremendous activity on many fronts – among scholars and the press. A world sensation was evident. News agencies, newspapers, radio and television spread the news to every corner of the earth.

But those who perhaps expected the Vasa to appear out of the muddy waters to be triumphantly towed in and placed below the palace for public viewing were perhaps disappointed. The step from finding to salvaging the ship was long and troublesome. Many significant questions had to be answered before the salvaging could even begin. What did the ship look like? Would the hull bear lifting? What would be done with the ship if it were salvaged? How could it be prevented from being destroyed by sun and wind when it did come up from the depth? From where would the money come for such a huge salvaging project? Who would pay for a museum building? And so on.

**The experienced head diver, Per Edvin Fälting,
played a decisive part in the salvage work,
in which with a sure hand and great authority he successfully
led the difficult and dangerous diving work.**

SALVAGE PREPARATIONS

PREPARING to salvage the old ship was a difficult assignment requiring practical seamanship, organisational talent, scholarly instincts and scientific ambitions. In February 1957, a special Wasa Committee was set up under the leadership of the head of the naval dockyard in Stockholm, Commander of the Fleet Edward Clason. The first task of this comprehensively composed committee was to investigate the technical and financial prerequisites for this complicated enterprise.

With exemplary speed, the naval authorities initiated the help needed to cope with the comprehensive preparatory work. It was decided that an essential part of naval diving training should be located to the Vasa. For the next few years, a large number of trainees on deep-sea diving courses and on revision courses for deep-sea divers had to become intimately acquainted with »The Old One«, as the Vasa's spirit came to be known with joking respect by the divers. As their leader, Chief Diver Per Edvin Fälting was appointed, a man of many years experience in his profession. At forty-eight, he had spent twelve thousand hours or in round figures six months underwater. He retired in 1976 after twenty eventful years in the service of the warship – after the salvaging, as head of the team of carpenters working on the restoration of the Vasa.

The all-overshadowing question was naturally whether it was possible to raise her. To find an answer to that question, the wreck had to be thoroughly inspected and measured. It was slowly established that the keel was slightly further down than a depth of thirty-five metres. On the port side of the Vasa the depth was twenty-nine to thirty metres and on the starboard side thirty-one to thirty-two. A considerable layer of silt, two to three metres thick, covered the firmer clay bottom. The relative large depth of water at the wreck contributed considerably to the difficulties. So that ascent times for the divers should not be too lengthy, it was usually necessary to limit working time down at the wreck to about half an hour. The ascent time is actually in direct proportion to the diving depth and diving time. As an example, a diver who has worked at a depth of thirty to thirty-three metres for thirty-five to fifty-five minutes has to take about forty-eight minutes ascending. For a diving time of twenty to thirty-five minutes to the same depth, no more than altogether seventeen minutes are needed for ascending.

Visibility down by the Vasa was very poor. Practically all light already disappears in the muddy waters of Strömmen at a depth of seven metres. On some days, with the help of thousand watt lights, the divers were able to see one and a half metres ahead of them at a depth of thirty metres. But as soon as the diver started working down in the depths, the silt swirled up around him in great clouds, making the lighting totally useless. Pollutants in the water reflect and scatter all light, so that all that can be seen is a greyish white wall ahead. The result is much the same as when the headlights of a car are shone into thick swirling snow or fog.

Because of the poor visibility, no one could see the whole of the Vasa. The divers had to feel their way ahead in the darkness over shattered decks, feeling gun-ports half-blocked with silt, glimpsing broken-off stumps of masts, sensing fantastic decorations and stumbling over loose finds beside the wreck. All observations were reported via telephone up to the diving boat and every report marked carefully on to sketches. Despite all this, both Fälting and his divers gradually became well acquainted with their wreck. The loudspeaker reports from the divers, fumbling their way down there in the dark, testify to this. This is what it might sound like: »I'm at point 4 and am walking astern, here is the collapsed transverse bulkhead. The forecastle ends here, yes, this is point 8.«

It was difficult to create a real picture of the old ship in this way. To achieve some kind of order in the pieces of the puzzle, the divers' investigations of the find had to be done strictly methodically. It soon turned out that some kind of reference system had to be found for all observations and measurements. This was done by stretching metre-graded plastic ribbons from the stems along the railings. No really accurate measurements were acquired in this way, but in the end the system turned out to fulfil its purpose. This measuring procedure took a whole month of diving, trying everyone's patience.

The second phase of the preparation began with checking all ship's deck beams, for their firmness and strength were to be of the greatest importance to the raising

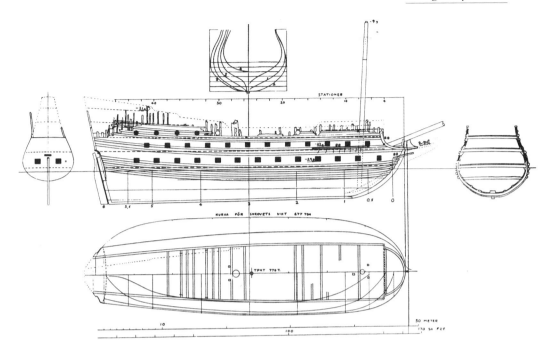

In 1957, Sam Svensson made the first reconstruction of the Vasa,
based mainly on the measurements taken by the divers and
available archive material. He also estimated the ship's centre mainpoint and
calculated the ship's weight under water to be about 750 tons,
which at the salvaging turned out to be surprisingly accurate.

of the wreck. It was easy to lose your way in the dimness down there. So that the divers could be sure they really were following the same beam across the ship, the beams were numbered clearly from stem to stern on both sides of the ship. This apparently simple method of checking required yet another month's work. With those measurements, it was also possible to establish that the ship had very little list to speak of.

Then the gun-ports were counted. Nor was this minor operation easy. »The number of gun-ports to starboard were first calculated to be 11 in the upper battery and 13 in the lower«, says the Wasa Committee in its report. »Later a 12th port was found to port in the upper level while the 13th cannot be found again. This may be due to the divers at the first count furthest astern confused the upper and lower levels. But it is not out of the question that there may be closed gun-ports that have evaded discovery. Until further notice, however, the distribution should be reckoned to be 12–12. Added to these are two ports in the stern at the lower level, one on each side of the sternpost.«

Time was racing on and it was already nearly the end of July, so it was considered urgent to complete as early as possible the examination of the silt-covered interior to the fore of the main mast of the ship, which was dredged out with the aid of a mammoth pump. This stage of the work also took a month. The dredging ceased at the end of August.

The intensive work of spring and summer had brought the Vasa team a good way towards attaining the dream of their aim – salvaging. There was a fairly clear idea of what the ship looked like, which was essential to know if the salvage operation was to be carried out. The committee was also able to add a sketch of the ship to their report, probably the very first drawing ever made of the Vasa.

Her length had been calculated to be fifty metres. The longest deck beams were eight metres between railing supports. The curve of the ship measured 1.85 metres on each side, and with the addition of the thickness of the railings, the ship's greatest width was about twelve metres. With the guidance of available old and new measurements, the Maritime Museum's skilled curator, Captain Sam Svensson, an experienced marine historian and schooner skipper, was able to calculate the Vasa's approximate weight. He established among other things that her displacement was about 1,300 tons and her weight about 750 tons as she lay there on the bottom of Strömmen.

It was now known that the hull was in a fairly good state, although the ship had suffered some damage over the course of the years. Another question of greatest importance had been answered, this time about the firmness of the material.

Examination had shown that the Vasa was very sturdily built. All parts of the ship which would be subject to strains at any eventual salvaging were made of oak, and apart from some surface softening, the timbers were in very good shape. But a chain is no stronger than its weakest link. The material used in the hull was indeed strong – but how were the various parts held together? It turned out that seven-teenth century shipbuilders had used both wood and iron to join the hull together. In the construction, altogether about 60,000 treenails of oak and juniper had been used. But in many places there were also iron joints in the form of ironwork, hinges and bolts. As far as could be seen, the iron had not fared as well as the timber, so it was an uncertain factor, doubly uncertain because the number of iron joints in the hull was not known.

According to information, about 50 people drowned when the Vasa sank. Altogether, the remains of 25 people were found in or alongside the ship.

SHE CAN BE SALVAGED

THE MOMENT of decision had arrived. Was it worth setting up a major salvaging apparatus to try to bring the ship up whole? Would she stand up to the huge strains of being lifted? Would the cables perhaps cut her to pieces or crush the hull and ruin all those highly tense expectations? Would it not be just as well to bring the Vasa up slowly bit by bit so as not to take any risks? This was no easy judgement, although all the investigations had shown that the Vasa was a sturdily built ship. As far as could be seen, there was nothing much wrong with her timbers, despite their three hundred years or so on the sea bed. It was also known that the timbers embedded in the clay had fared best and the treenails used had considerable holding strength.

The Timber Research Institute eventually also produced a statement which supported the committee in its view that the Vasa could be salvaged. The Institute also maintained the oak's strength against bending, strain and pressure had only been reduced by about forty per cent. On the other hand the impact resistance was roughly seventy-five per cent worse than in fresh oak. So the examination results were tested, argued over, calculated, weighed for and against until it was considered salvaging could be recommended.

The choice of salvage method also gave rise to a number of speculations. One of the possibilities discussed was placing an appropriate number of large nylon or synthetic rubber balloons inside the hull. These would then be inflated from a pumping station on the surface. The American Navy had used this method when salvaging ships sunk during the atomic bomb tests in Bikini Atoll in 1946. The experiment with balloons was successful, and such balloons with a lifting strength of 15, 25 and 40 tons are produced. The system seemed seductively simple. But the proposers had not really thought through the actual problem. The balloon method would entail exactly what the committee wished to avoid, namely that great force would be directed from the interior and outwards. Ships are, after all, built to resist powerful pressure from the outside.

So there was much to be said for the use of more conventional salvaging methods. With those, work can be carried out with pontoons and strong wires or slings, and in three principle different ways. Now it was a matter of which of them should be used. A sunken ship can, for instance, be lifted with the aid of large cylinders of air which are filled with water and sunk beside the wreck. The cylinders are fastened with chains and cables to the ship's sides, and when the water is pressed out of the cylinders by compressed air, they float up and take the ship with them to the surface. The lifting takes place in one stage and the possibilities of controlling what happens down below with this method are fairly small.

When it came to the Vasa, it was of the greatest importance to be able constantly to control events under the water. That possibility is considerably greater with the other two methods. Then large lifting pontoons with considerable lifting power are used. They are filled with water so that their decks are almost level with the surface of the water. The powerful lifting cables, which have been eased under the wreck, are then fastened to the pontoons and when all the preparations have been made, the water is pumped out. The pontoons rise, taking the wreck with them. Secondary vessels, the disabled boat and pontoons are then towed in to shallower waters. Once the wreck is aground, the pontoons are again sunk, the lifting cables tautened and the pontoons emptied. Then lift after lift has to be carried out until the disabled craft is in place.

The third method entails hydraulic lifting arrangements or jacks to carry out the lifting work. On the pontoons are stands for these jacks, with which the ship can be »pumped up« in one stage.

The successive method of lift after lift required careful reconnaisance of the fairway, so that stones, wrecks or other larger obstacles would not damage the valuable ship. The pontoons would also have to be able to lift the Vasa out of the deep hollow in which she had rested for so many years.

One of the disadvantages of the jacking method was that it needed especially thick lifting cables with clumsy linking arrangements. These could turn out to be troublesome to get under the ship. The distance between the farthest astern and farthest fore jacks on the available lifting pontoons was only twenty-four metres. This was an essential inconvenience. The length of the Vasa had been estimated as fifty metres and large parts of the ship would then come to hang outside the support of the bearing cables. The risk that these overhanging parts would break was great. The committee finally decided to choose the stage-by-stage method. If this should turn out to be inappropriate, it would be simpler to get the heavier slings under the Vasa if she had already been raised a little and was hanging in the lighter lifting cables.

While speculations round the choice of lifting method and the bearing strength of the wreck etc went on, the work on the old ship continued indefatigably. At the end of August, 1957, they started »digging« the first cable tunnel. That also proved to be no easy task. First, the Vasa was lying rather unfortunately just outside the gates to the largest dry dock in Stockholm – Gustav V Dock. At the end of the summer, the traffic to and from the dock became increasingly lively. Every time a ship was to go in or out, work on the Vasa had to stop and the diving rafts towed away. While the dredging pump was working in order to get down to the firmer clay bottom, a number of loose finds were discovered. Thus the tunnelling work was even further delayed, as the finds naturally had to be freed and looked after. A number of interesting objects had already been salvaged from the depths, among them the broken-off foremast brought up in November 1956. Right up to December, the divers continued with the difficult tunnelling work. By then they had got as far as to the keel, so it was considered evident that it was technically possible to make a salvage attempt.

Extremely valuable and inspiring help had already been promised in 1956 by the Neptune Company, which offered its services free to place the pontoons *Oden* and *Frigg* and also the necessary number of salvage vessels at the disposal of the project. The conditions for this generous offer were two, one that the Vasa should be lifted whole and preserved, and secondly that the lifting work should take place under the direction of the company and in the charge of the company's experienced salvage expert, Captain Axel Hedberg.

Another generous offer came from Fagersta Bruk AB, who promised to supply free of charge the twelve one-hundred-and-twenty metre long six inch cables needed for the lifting.

Among the earliest finds was the Vasa's figurehead,
a roaring lion leaping ahead, gold leaf still glittering
in the carefully carved mane.

THE DIVERS' MASTER-TEST

By the middle of April 1958, work again began out at the Vasa. Everything was in fine trim for the coming season. During the summer, the naval divers were to show what they could do, now a matter of burrowing their way under the keel in tunnel after tunnel through silt and clay, all in compact darkness.

Air and water were the only aids the divers had. The equipment was a Zetterström jet and an airlift, also called mammoth-pump with a suction tube. The water jet was the »spade« while the airlift with its suction tube largely functioned like a gigantic vacuum cleaner.

The Zetterström jet nozzle works with a water jet cutting forwards through the clay, at the same time pressing water backwards, thus making the device recoil-less. According to need, the diver can regulate the distribution of water. The backwards flow must not be too strong, for then silt and clay are easily washed past the suction mouthpiece and cutting strength is reduced.

A diver's ordinary working day on the diving float can be as follows:

One of the navy's »hard-hat« divers has just received his instructions from Fälting on board the diving boat lying above the Vasa. The dressing procedure has recently been gone through, the diving suit and its accessories weighing almost a hundred kilos. Sturdy gear and warm clothes are needed to cope with work at a depth of about thirty-five metres, where the temperature is no higher than four degrees Celsius. Strong woollen clothing protects the diver against the cold and against chafing from the diving suit, or the »clothing«, made of strong cotton cloth with a rubber lining. The clothing is usually in one piece and the diver wriggles into it from the top, rubber cuffs at his wrists making it watertight. Round his neck are two collars, the outer one of strong rubber and watertight, which is joined to what is called the breastplate. The heavy diving boots with their thick lead soles are already on, the diver's knife suspended in his belt ready for use. One of his colleagues brings the uncomfortable big copper helmet and eases it over the diver's head, then the helmet is carefully screwed down to the breastplate. The inlet for the air tube, a regulating valve and the join for the telephone cable are on the helmet. The diver can regulate the air intake in his suit through the regulating valve, so a skilled diver is able to adjust the air intake so that he floats freely in the water.

The signalling cable with its inbuilt telephone line is fixed firmly round his waist and his air tube is clear. The front window of the helmet is screwed down and the air intake and telephone communication tested for one last time. A slap on the helmet is the all clear sign. The diver starts his descent along the basic line leading straight down to his workplace about thirty-five metres beneath the diving boat, taking the spool hose with him. It grows dark very quickly on the way down. Everything becomes green, greyish-green, dirty brown, darker...dark, so dark that the diver is as good as blind. He comes to the shaft his colleagues have dug for roughly five metres straight into the silt and clay. The tunnel curves inwards here. Slowly and carefully, the diver makes his way down and inwards. He is in the tunnel's horizontal section and feels his way towards the place where one of his colleagues a moment ago has stopped working at the end of his stint.

On the diving boat, Fälting is attentively following his pupil. The depth measure shows thirty-seven metres. The diver's voice and breathing can constantly be heard in the telephone and from his voice it can almost be heard that he is in distress and lonely. Nor is it entirely without risks down there. But the work goes on, for the Zetterström nozzle is effective. Clay swirls loose and is sucked into the coarse mammoth tube, which comes out on the deck of a barge where the flow of water is thoroughly examined. Occasionally a loose find comes up with the flow of silt and clay.

Bit by bit, the diver works his way ahead. He works face down, his head occasionally hitting something hard, the bottom of the Vasa, her 750 ton heavy hull just above the diver's head. How strong really is the hull – how much ballast is lying there above the bottom planks? It is a horrible job, testing the nerves and a strain on the body. But it has to be done if she is to be brought up. Six tunnels from side to side – each one nearly twenty-five metres long – have to be dug out if she is to be raised. Altogether, that means one hundred and fifty metres of tunnel at a depth of thirty-five to forty metres have to be completed before the lifting cables can be eased under the hull and up to the lifting pontoons.

The tunnels under the Vasa were dug with Zetter-ström's nozzle sending a concentrated jet of water to wash away the mud. The mud was taken away by the jet collar, which also kept the nozzle recoil-free.

Lying in a narrow tunnel, and in total darkness working your way underneath the Vasa was stressful work for the divers. The mud washed away was sucked by a pump up to the surface for sieving and checking.
Drawing by Bengt Wallén.

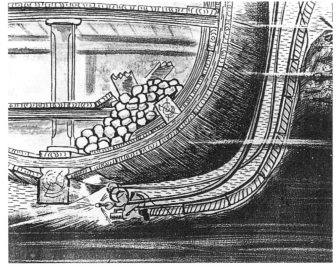

Almost until Christmas, work on the Vasa continued during 1958. Since the spring of 1957, when the systematic work was begun, almost a thousand dives had been completed. That had meant many hours of preparations, many hours of waiting at various depths during the ascent after hard work in silt and clay round »the Old One's nest«.

**The strain on the cables was great when the Vasa was raised.
This meant they narrowed slightly, and so the nuts of the cable locks
had to be tightened at regular intervals.**

THE SALVAGE FLEET ARRIVES

ANOTHER spring dawns, the third for the Vasa, and it was now 1959. Optimism with an undertone of anxiety about the future probably marked the mood of the team faced with this decisive season. New divers from the navy were to go through their baptism of mud beneath the ship. The tunnelling was to continue with what that entailed of pressure on the nerves and physical strain, as well as the demands made on professional skills and personal courage. The season's work was to provide the Swedish Navy divers with a top place in the international diving world, where their achievements were being watched with much excitement and interest.

It is hard to form a whole picture of what was really being carried out in connection with this utterly unique salvage enterprise. Complicated salvage and diving jobs have certainly been carried out all over the world. Both Swedish and foreign salvage vessels have coped with many apparently impossible operations. Salvage vessels have struggled in bad weather and high seas to save ships and men from serious situations. Divers have been down to great depths and brought up many valuable objects that had gone to the bottom with the ship. Sunken ships have been raised on open coasts, and harbours have been cleared of hundreds of wrecks lost in wartime. Human lives and valuable property have been hazarded in various salvage operations. It is the salvager's lot to work in silence, his everyday job often hard and thankless, occasionally profitable, but extremely rarely easy. Despite everything previously achieved in the world of salvaging, nonetheless the Vasa enterprise is unique.

Normally, working on ships concerns vessels about which everything is known.

There are complete blueprints of the hull and interior details, and dimensions of ribs and plating, keel and floor are all known, as well as what the material will stand and what strains it can be exposed to without breaking. Stowing plans for cargo and verbal decriptions from officers and crew complement the picture of the wreck. Salvage material and methods are also adapted to ships of today.

When it came to the Vasa, everything was different. She was very old and there were no blueprints. Such things did not begin to come into use until the end of the eighteenth century. From the start, nothing was known of the quality or strength of the materials. Some parts of the hull could be examined, others not. The heavy stone ballast could not be taken out, as it was impossible to get down into the ship. The centre main point of the ship was also uncertain, nor was her exact underwater weight known. Silt, clay and wretched visibility, irritating boat traffic and much else all constantly created new difficulties. The lack of knowledge of the Vasa's power of resistance also meant that they were forced to choose roundabout methods of salvaging. Had they been certain from the start that the old ship was as tough as she later turned out to be, then they could have chosen a quicker way of salvaging her. Now they had to follow the much lengthier and more troublesome road of caution and care.

Enthusiasm, pleasure in the work and team spirit urged the salvage team on into almost superhuman efforts. So it was a day of triumph when the lifting cables were at last in place under the ship, ready to be extended up to the big lifting pontoons. The time had come. Would three years of intensive work turn out to have been in vain, or would things go according to plan?

On August 13th, the units of the salvage fleet began to arrive. Above the wreck were anchored the Neptune Company's two pontoons, *Oden* and *Frigg*, with a joint lifting power of 2,400 tons. They did not look up to much, but are typical working platforms, and as such very effective. At the same time, they are a strange craft. Their task simply consists of being filled with water, then being emptied again. As the lifting cables are fixed when the pontoons are filled with water, the sunken ship rises with them as the water is pumped out, i.e. as long as the ship is not too heavy or is adhering firmly to the seabed. The pontoons have no steam power of their own, so steam for their powerful pumps has to be delivered from a ship alongside.

The fleet also included the Neptune Company's salvage ships, the *Sleipner* and the *Atlas*, as well as the Navy's tender, the *Sprängaren* (the Blaster). Immediately above the Vasa were two concrete pontoons and the dockyard's well-equipped diving boat.

**Three models donated by the Neptune Salvage Company
show how the salvaging was carried out.**

The workforce now amounted to about sixty professional men. The work was going smoothly and methodically under Captain Hedberg's sure leadership. The lifting cables were taken up and fastened one by one in such a way that the pontoons should not list during the lifting. All the cables had to be exactly equally taut so as not to jeopardize the whole enterprise. Sturdy gear was needed for lifting about seven hundred tons, the weight Captain Sam Svensson had calculated the Vasa to be under the water. He had also calculated the approximate position of the ship's centre main point, and it turned out later that this experienced seaman's calculations were astonishingly accurate.

The lifting cables donated by Fagersta Bruk had impressive dimensions, each cable a hundred and twenty-five metres long and able to bear a load of an equal number of tons. The diameter of the cables was five centimetres. The cable locks were large pieces weighing fifty-seven kilos each, so tautening and locking the cables was hard work.

The entire salvage armada was moored and anchored with great thoroughness so that it lay safely in place. Light buoys round the salvage site warned ships and boats to keep away. Over the radio, information for seafaring and daily papers were publicised directions on speed limits round the workplace. There were also appeals in various ways to the leisure-time sailing public to observe the greatest caution when sailing through the area, as their wash might well jeopardize the whole venture. The final preparations took a week – a week in which tensions kept rising.

Then came the first of the »lift days« – Thursday August 20th, 1959. On board the salvage fleet, activity began early. The lifting cables were given a final inspection while divers checked that all was apparently well down with the Vasa. The guard boats were slowly patrolling round the site, stopping boats going too fast, and turning away the all-too curious. Sightseeing boats of tourists passed full of people wanting to catch a glimpse of the operation, and the salvage fleet's motor-boats provided a shuttle service for prominent people and the press. Everyone was equally expectant. At about half past eleven, all the cables were tautened, all in all nearly fifteen hundred metres of steel hawser now in slings round the Vasa.

The awaited moment of tension and wonder, hope and doubt had come. Soon after lunch, the pontoons' pumps began working and involuntarily, voices were lowered a trifle. Everyone was waiting for the sensation and everyone had to be respectfully quiet to notice it. A slight tremble in the hull of the pontoons and a hissing jet of steam from the pumps were the only signs that anything was really happening. Slowly and cautiously the two pontoons were relieved of ton after ton.

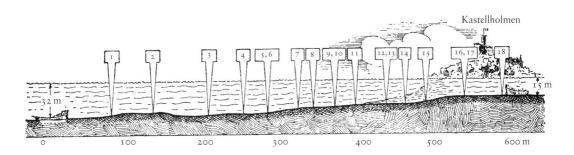

DATE	LIFT NO.	APPROX. HEIGHT GAIN	NOTES
August			
20	1	2 m	Vasa sheered 180 degrees to starboard and set down 100 m closer to Kastellholmen.
21	2	2 m	Vasa tips forward with 12 degree list to port.
22	–	–	Divers establish minor abrasions by cables.
24	3	0.5 m	Vasa turned stern first.
25	4	0.5 m	Adjustment of cables.
26	5	1 m	26 m depth to sea bed.
27	–	–	Still for stiff west wind.
28	6	1 m	Half stretch to Kastellholmen covered.
31	7	–	Sea bed looser than calculated.
September			
1	–	–	Adjustment of cables.
2	Incompleted lift.		Vasa not over edge of hollow.
3	–	–	Adjustment of cables.
4	8	1 m	Vasa placed across hollow.
7	–	–	Adjustment of cables. 12 degrees port list.
8	9 *and* 10	1 m	Two lifts. Stem towards Kastellholmen.
9	11	0.5 m	Cables in place.
10	12 *and* 13	1 m	Two lifts.
11	14	1 m	Stem towards Gröna Lund.
14	15	1 m	Further towards Gröna Lund.
15	16 *and* 17	1 m	Two lifts, 18 m depth of water.
16	18	2 m	Lowering to 16 m depth of water midwaters between Kastellholmen and Djurgårdslandet.

After about twenty minutes, the leader of the operation said: »The lifting power is now a hundred tons. We'll soon be able to continue to two hundred tons.«

The cables were already taut. The time had come to tighten the nuts on the cable locks, for the huge load had made the cables narrow slightly.

Crowds of people had gathered on the heights of Söder and all round Slussen, in the same way as they had once before in time to witness the brief maiden voyage of the Vasa. The population of Stockholm had roughly increased a hundredfold since then. The seventeenth century sensation, however, must have been considerably greater than this one today. It was a quiet, almost discreet event which the general public was experiencing. At first there was almost nothing to be seen on the pontoons. The dramatic tug-of-war between the Vasa and the constellation of *Oden-Frigg* was being played out in the dark depths below the spectators. But down there, it would have been difficult to experience anything of the great drama of the first lift.

»You might just as well go into a dark wardrobe and feel a piece of wet wood,« a diver said to a journalist wanting to go down there to see for himself.

Calmly and methodically, the routine checks of cables and locks were made. Soundings of the depth of water in the pontoons were taken at regular intervals. The free divers sat watchfully on a raft, gazing intently at the floats and the main cables fasteneed fore and aft to the Vasa to show whether she was moving. After an hour or so, the pontoon on the starboard side of the Vasa began to lift slightly, more than the rise of the port pontoon. A moment or two later, the port pontoon began to list towards the wreck. The pontoons had also now moved closer to each other.

It is quite natural that the port pontoon is listing inwards, the experts said. When the Vasa sank, she had the wind to starboard, so she listed to port. The ballast had probably slipped when the ship capsized and a large part of it presumably rolled over to the port side, where it is probably still lying, so the Vasa is heavier to port than to starboard, although she is almost upright.

The pumps went on working. By a quarter to three, they had reached to over 400 tons lifting strength, by half past three 600 tons, and by ten past four up to 700 tons. Half an hour later, the pumping was stopped. The time had come. Would the weight calculations be right? According to them, she was to weigh about seven hundred tons under the water. Everything was going so smoothly, so quietly. Nothing unexpected was happening. The cables were as taut as violin strings, testifying to the tug-of-war going on down there. The clay had no real desire to let go its hold. But water had now begun to trickle in between the wreck and the clay bed, so the suction of the vacuum was slowly but surely being reduced. Suddenly, the main cable slackened slightly and the floats began to move very slightly.

At last the time had come to send down a diver to find out what was happening down below. Chief Diver Fälting gave his last instructions. The helmet was screwed on. The telephone and loudspeaker connections were tested and, chatting, diver Sven Olof Nyberg went down. A moment later came his timely words: »I am at the bottom now and can feel the sternpost. The Vasa has risen four to five decimetres according to my measurements. Some splinters have come off. The cables seem to have cut off a few planks, otherwise she seems all right.«

At about eight that evening, the pontoons had been emptied of all water. The ship was up out of the hollow she had been resting in for almost exactly three hundred and thirty-one years. Her trip to her next resting place could begin. At first the entire salvaging armada was swung round so that the precious suspended load came transversely across the hollow. Once this turn had been accomplished, towing began. About a hundred metres had been covered when the Vasa touched bottom and was carefully lowered again.

All told, the Vasa's scarcely six hundred metre long voyage lasted for twenty-eight days. The distances per day were short, but nevertheless forward and upwards despite troubles of various kinds. On the whole, one day was much like the next for the men of the salvaging team. The same constant grinding hard work – trying to their patience and sometimes even a trifle monotonous according to a timetable as follows: the Vasa was towed towards shallower water until she touched bottom. Then *Oden* and *Frigg* were slowly filled with water so that the ship could settle properly on the sea bed. The cables were tautened and locked. The pontoons were emptied again and the Vasa lifted about four metres. Another tow, another touching the bottom, then the whole procedure was repeated over and over again. As it was lowered, the Vasa sometimes sank over three metres into the sea bed sediment, so the netto lifting height on some occasions became equal to zero.

At first the ship was towed with the prow foremost, but after a few days this turned out to be inappropriate. The Vasa was heavy and wide to the fore and at every touch down on the seabed, the ship shovelled huge masses of clay in front of her, digging herself down to an abnormal extent. So on the third lift, it was decided to turn her and continue the trip with the more pointed stern foremost. When the Vasa was lifted for the first time, she was listing by ten to twelve degrees, and she was also slightly tipped forward. However, these details were corrected at an early stage.

It was slippery going uphill, where mud and silt made moving very much more difficult. During the tow, the cables slipped and the divers had some difficulty getting them back into place. But no particularly serious intermezzo occurred in connection with the first stage of salvaging the Vasa. Bad weather did force the salvage fleet to be still for a day, but this involuntary waiting period was used for various diving jobs, among others straightening the cables and also running yet another cable under the ship.

Towards the end of the climb uphill towards shallower water, the lifts had to be carried out with the utmost caution, so that the Vasa did not strike the pontoons. On one or two occasions, the nerves of the salvage team were sorely tried, when boats and ships almost sailed straight into the confusion of tow ropes and anchor cables. But all went well, and on the afternoon of Wednesday, September 16th, the first stage could be reported to have been completed after eighteen lifts.

Up to that date, the warship had helped to provide the Navy with a professional diving élite which in a worthy manner had completed this pioneer deed that had been begun in the seventeenth century. Despite difficult circumstances and the risks inevitably taken, no fewer than thirteen hundred dives had been made without a single accident, a good testimony to the quality and professional skill of the leader of the divers' training.

Per Edvin Fälting and his assistants were officially commended, a total of 25 divers from the navy and the coastal artillery, at a formal occasion a few days after the Vasa had reached her new resting place. The head of the navy, Admiral Stig H:son Ericson, handed over the Vasa medal to Fälting, and the divers were awarded the navy's medal for professional skills. On the back of the medal was engraved: *For skill in diving at the salvaging of the Vasa.* That was the first time it had been awarded for diving services. The title of Vasa-Diver had become a title of honour.

THE FIRST FINDS

URING the three years the salvaging preparations were taking place, a great
many interesting finds were brought to the surface, and by the autumn of
1959 the catalogue of finds contained all told about eight hundred items.
Primarily, tunnelling activities produced various objects of different kinds. At first
curiosity was aroused by a series of finds of which several were of less interest to the
general public. Number one on the list, for instance, is »Pine plank, round on one
side, flat on the other. Length 9.80 m. Width 55 cm, tapering.« The ship's foremast
had already been found in November 1959, a slimy, almost twenty metres long,
coarse green spar, broken below the top. The upper part of the lower mast was
found later, and then it was possible to establish that its total length was twenty-
four and a half metres, its diameter at deck height seventy-two centimetres.

But it was not long before more spectacular finds were brought up from the silt
tomb round the Vasa. A series of wonderfully beautiful sculptures soon produced
evidence that the ship had been a magnificent vessel. Art historians compared her
with Jakob de la Gardie's extravagantly decorated Stockholm palace, Makalös
(Peerless), completed in 1639. No one had any idea that so much knowledge of art
history could be found in a seventeenth century ship. According to the Skepps-
gården accounts, several master-carvers were employed to give the ship a worthy
decor. For his work, Carver Mårten signed for 354 riksdaler, Carver Hans 129
daler and Carver Gert 97 daler and 16 öre. More modest fees were earned by Johan
Thessen and Carver Petter. In 1626, the king also brought in from abroad a wood-
carver called Marcus Ledens. Master Mårten was identical with the famous
Mårten Redtmer, whose work included the pulpit in Jacob's Church and the legen-

73

dary copper figure that once stood as a symbol of punishment in Stortorget in the Old City and is today in the Stockholm Law Courts.

A singular cavalcade of fair mermaids, stern warriors, horrible dragons and other figures rose out of Strömmen. It must have taken considerable time to have achieved all the elaborate figures and groups of figures now being collected in the store-rooms on land. Quite early on, a curved headrail from the beak-head was found, and later some double-sided sculptured ornaments, among them a prone figure with a flapping cloak and a bird with a wriggling snake in its beak. It turned out later that they were part of a suite of sculptures depicting the ancient Greek legend of Peleus' battle against Thetis, Goddess of the Sea. The divers also found a metre-high statue of a Roman and his laurel wreath. A banderol at the foot of the statue bore the inscription »Tiberius«. The Roman Emperor gradually acquired eighteen colleagues, all of them part of the beak-head adornment.

The Vasa and the salvaged objects soon told a great deal about seventeenth century shipbuilding, including interesting information on the construction and thickness of planking. The Vasa is carvel-built with about six and a half to seven centimetres thick oak planks. Carvel-building entails the planks being jammed tightly against each other, so that the outer surface of the hull is even. Inside the planking are frame timbers and filling timbers, covered on the inside with the planks of the inner ceiling. The total thickness of the ship's sides has in some places been measured to about half a metre. Along what is called the wales, the side is even thicker. It was also possible to conclude from the finds the way certain decorative details were painted. The insides of the gun-port lids showed traces of having been painted red, while the lion masks adorning them were painted yellow with gaping red mouths, white teeth and whites of eyes.

The ship's rudder was salvaged at the end of November 1958. A great many experts gathered to watch as Stockholm City's great pontoon crane *Lodbrok* was to lift the three ton piece. The rudder is 10.3 metres long and made from two oak timbers with a combined width of 1.4 metres. The rudder blade is about four decimetres thick. The surface of the rudder, however, is relatively small and when steering the greatest angle was about 20 degrees each way.

There was particular excitement in September 1958 when one of the ship's guns was salvaged. The piece had been lying in the furthest astern gun-port, to port in the lower battery. As it was in the way of the salvage work and also kept threatening to slide out of the gun-port, it was considered safest to bring it up. *Lodbrok* lowered its lifting arm over the find and soon a three metre long, beautiful green-shimmering bronze piece was hovering above the surface of the water. The experts

**The roaring lion that had been the figurehead of the Vasa
has over the centuries become somewhat toothless.
The protruding tongue was found on later dives.**

registered the piece as a short 24-pounder gun of about 14,8 cm calibre. The Vasa carried altogether 64 guns, of which forty-eight were 24-pounders. The combined weight of her artillery was about 80 tons.

When the gun was given its first rinsing, it could be seen that the rear part of the ornamentation had been damaged by a moulding fault. But nonetheless, the emblem of the Vasa dynasty, the stylised sheaf, was clearly distinguishable. On the sides were two lift-mountings, so-called dolphins, here as figures of wolves. On the chamber-piece the letters GARS can be read, and the numbers 162, the last number in the date illegible. The piece, like most of the Vasa's guns, was probably made at the »cannon foundry« near the present Brunkebergstorg. The boring and polishing of the pieces were done later at the Admiralty boring mill and polishing house, which took their power from Norrström.

Metal tests on the pieces done for the Maritime Museum have been analysed by the Svenska Metallverken laboratories in Västerås. At the same time, tests were also examined from a gun from the ship *Riksnyckeln*, salvaged in 1920. The analyses reinforced the presumption that the copper in the guns had been taken from Falu copper mines. They were also able to establish that after moulding, the guns were made white hot to strengthen them. If an interpretation of the coating in the bore of the Vasa's gun is accurate, no shot was ever fired from it.

The impressive lion which constituted the ship's figurehead caused a great sensation. This was one of the last finds made before the Vasa was raised, a splendid lion taking a great leap at the evil enemy. The lion – three metres and twenty-five centimetres long, sixty-five centimetres wide and almost a metre high – was lifted out of the water directly on land at Beckholmen. As the water from the fire-hose washed over the figurehead, it started glittering slightly with gold in the lion's mane.

As the ship set out on her maiden voyage, she represented a seventeenth century society in miniature. On board was what people of the day needed for survival. Stores for provisions contained food and drink, in the magazines were cannonballs and gunpowder, in the stock stores equipment of all kinds, sails, hand weapons, tools and cordage. The crew kept their personal belongings in chests and barrels. Even a pewter bottle was found, containing a still tasty rum-like, 33% alcohol drink.

However, the main aim of the first three years of work was not to pick up loose articles, but to try to raise the whole ship. The loose finds turned out to be both to the good and the bad – they did stimulate interest in the Vasa, but at the same time they delayed the salvage work. The conserving of the many articles was a time-

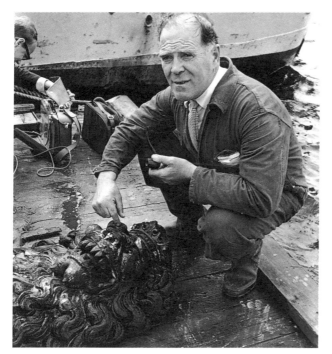

In September 1958, one of the three remaining 24-pounder guns was raised in the presence of a large crowd out on the salvage site.

In connection with the tunnel clearing and the preparations for the first lifting, the divers occasionally found new and impressive carvings from the Vasa's decorations. Here is one of the two lions holding shields that were part of the Swedish coat-of-arms. The national coat-of-arms was a central part of the decoration of the stern.

Two carvings were found representing Hercules,
one as a young and the other as an old man. This is the elderly Hercules,
draped in a lion's skin and with the hound of hell Cerberus at his feet.

One of six knights in armour who were on guard
round the Admiral's cabin windows in the stern.

consuming, expensive and troublesome procedure that had to be carried out with piety and great care if they were not to be damaged.

The Wasa Committee was re-formed in a letter from the king on September 30th, 1959 to the Wasa Commission. The chairman of the Commission became Prince Bertil, and Carl-Albert Andersson, chairman of of Stockholm City Council, became vice-chairman. The Commission was given the task of handling all future salvage work and also producing proposals for how the final running and exhibiting of the Vasa was to be done. The Commission functioned up until July 1st, 1964, when the Wasa Shipyard was merged with the National Maritime Museum.

One of the two Tritons included in the lintel above the door to the main cabin.

One of the two lions holding shields
included in the national coat-of-arms in the stern.
Traces of gold leaf bearing witness to their earlier magnificence
were found at the salvaging.

ON TOWARDS THE FINAL LIFT

P ER EDVIN FÄLTING and his divers still had to spend a great many strenuous hours down in the Vasa. Out on the disaster site, the exciting and dangerous tunnelling had long been the dominant occupation. Now tasks of quite a different nature awaited the diving team. First and foremost, it was necessary to clear the upper battery deck of silt, dross and ash, stones and old anchors which over the years had accumulated there. But they had to go carefully with the clearing, first and foremost not to damage valuable finds that might be lying under all the rubbish. For the final preparations, the divers were also able to manage carpentry work under the water. Seventeenth century divers had been rather rough when salvaging the ship's guns. Over the centuries, the damage done by them had been perpetuated by ships and boats quite unknowingly anchoring on the old ship. Some captains certainly must have sworn black and blue at the unknown object that had robbed them of good anchors. Almost forty anchors of various sizes and from different epochs that had fastened into the Vasa's hull testified to this. It is truly amazing that the Vasa was in as good shape as she was. It was known that the high sterncastle had collapsed, as well as that a vessel had some time in 1958 been forced in thick fog to anchor in an emergency in the Vasa, thus completing the destruction of the sterncastle.

Before the salvaging, the Vasa had to be made as watertight as possible. So under water, divers had to attempt to construct a replacement of the collapsed sterncastle. This alone entailed that those down in the mirky depths had to achieve a building corresponding to smallish well-built watertight barn. On top of that, they had to strengthen the hull athwartships so that it could resist the strains of the lifting through the surface of the water. This reinforcement was carried out with iron rods linked together three by three and pulled through two opposite gun-ports. There, the iron rods were tightened with nuts against iron girders placed outside the hull. Four athwartship reinforcements of that kind were arranged. In addition, all the gun-ports had to be closed up with effective sealing. A troublesome task was also sealing the thousands of holes from the rusted-away iron bolts which had once contributed to giving the great hull its strength and durability, monotonous work demanding great patience, and despite the reduced depth, visibility was still wretched.

In the late summer of 1960, routine work was interrupted when the eleventh International Historical Congress was held in Stockholm, and what could be more natural than inviting the roughly 2,000 delegates at the congress to a special showing? This meant that for about an hour the Vasa was the focus of attention for about forty million television watchers in eight countries. A lively drama developed in the area round the warship. The accumulated expertise of historians and heraldic experts from all over the world were given an opportunity to watch at close quarters the salvaging of a ship's anchor, a gun carriage and the second gun to be salvaged from the Vasa in modern times. One of the interesting elements in the programme was a realistic demonstration of a diving bell of the kind von Treileben had used in the seventeenth century.

In the summer of 1960, a nation-wide collection was begun for funds for the Vasa project, and Svenska Handelsbanken opened accounts all over the country for the sale of a specially minted Wasa coin. About six months later, the bank was able to hand a million kronor over to the chairman of this new foundation called Wasa Rediviva.

Intensive preparatory work continued during extended working days up to July. The weather was unusually favourable with the mildest winter Stockholm had experienced for many years. So everything went roughly according to plan, occasionally even well ahead of schedule.

Alongside the practical work out at the Vasa, the commission's many consultants and other experts were preparing for what was to come next. The project still had many difficult and uncertain factors, the main question still remaining: would it be possible to carry out the enterprise or not? Would they dare draw up a definite time schedule? Timetables are not exactly common in connection with salvaging operations, in which unpredictable events can easily throw the most well thought-out plans, but the eyes of the world were on the Vasa and people were beginning to expect more details of the final phase of the project.

All this complicated work at times created a certain amount of irritation, and

The contours of the Vasa's hull can clearly be seen in the water
between the salvage pontoons.
The last Vasa lift is about to be completed.

meanwhile serious dissension arose between the partners involved. Towards the end of 1960, the management of the Neptune Company threatened to withdraw from the entire project. What might have happened then does not bear thinking about. However, after considerable discussion just before Christmas, a preliminary timetable was at last been agreed on. According to this, all preparatory work was to be finished by April 4th, 1961, when the salvage fleet would be anchored above the Vasa. No one dared yet definitely decide on a date for the raising, though a day during the period between April 20th and 27th was selected. Although all the work done during the autumn and winter had produced no dramatic events or interesting finds, interest in the general public continued to rise. Instinctively, excitement could be felt in the air.

After a well-deserved Christmas and New Year break, the Vasa team again started work at the beginning of January by sealing, shoring up and reinforcing the hull. Optimism slowly but surely increased, and even the most cautious began to be fairly convinced that the Vasa would come up – but no one could be totally certain until the salvaging was a completed fact. The uncertainty itself contributed to a great extent to making the whole project exciting. Despite this, it gradually became necessary to plan seriously and start the costly building activities required for the Vasa in time to have a worthy and purposeful, if provisional museum. The building and material sections of the commission were given more and more to do, and the archaeological group was working intensively on planning their activities. Great demands were to be made on the chief archaeologist, Per Lundström, and his colleagues, for no one had ever previously carried out a similar assignment. They had no other previous experience to draw on for their plans, and they knew very little about the interior of the Vasa or what might be found in her. The conservation experts also had various problems to wrestle with at this time of speculation and uncertainty.

In the middle of March 1961, the Navy put a number of assault divers at the project's disposal and with their help the nearly 6,000 wooden plugs needed to seal the holes left by the rusted-away iron bolts in the Vasa's solid oak sides had been hammered in. The heavy diver team had now also been complemented by some experienced professional civilian divers. April 4th was approaching rapidly. Per Edvin Fälting and his men, however, were able to await the arrival of the salvage fleet with equinimity. Their preparations were complete.

**Monday, April 24th, 1961. Early in the morning,
people begin to make their way out to Kastellholmen
to ensure themselves a good place from which to watch the final lift.**

**The first view of the Vasa are the ribs
sticking in ragged rows above the water.**

OUT OF THE DEPTHS

O N APRIL 4th, 1961, the Neptune Company's two salvage ships the *Atlas* and the *Ajax*, arrived at the site and were anchored safely together with the *Sleipner* by the Vasa, where the *Oden* and the *Frigg* were also in place, the Navy's submarine salvage ship, the *Belos*, complementing the fleet. All told, seventy or so men were working under Captain Axel Hedberg's experienced leadership. The following day, representatives of the press, radio and television had been invited to a press conference, and were at last to be told what the coming period entailed. The weather was grey and cold, the wind blowing rather coldly on this international gathering, while the experts on the deck of the *Sleipner* described the course of events of the operation.

»If all goes according to our calculations,« stated the salvage leader, »the Vasa will break through the surface of the water for the first time after 333 years on a day between April 20th and the 27th. The exact moment in time has hitherto been impossible to decide. Immediately afterwards, the work will continue on sealing the Vasa and reinforcing the hull wherever it is considered necessary. The archaeologists will be brought in at an early stage to help lighten the ship and if possible right the present list. A very important detail in the work will be the pumping her free of water, which will also be begun immediately after the lifting. As soon as the Vasa is floating sufficiently high in the water to be able to cross the entrance of the Gustav V dock, the intention is to take the ship there. This is reckoned to occur one day during the first half of May.

»In dry dock, the Vasa is to be placed on a concrete pontoon at present being built at Gävle Shipyard. The pontoon would be one of the largest of its kind ever built in Sweden. It is 56 metres long, 21 metres wide, almost 4 metres high and can bear a weight of 2,000 tons.« The building of the pontoon otherwise constituted one of the many telling proofs of the great interest taken by Swedish industry in the Vasa project. Free of charge, Gävle Shipyard provided the project with its new 100 metre long floating dock, in which the building of the pontoon was carried out by an organisation formed especially for the purpose.

The two pontoons, the *Oden* and the *Frigg*, were now the main characters round the Vasa for the second time, built in 1898 to salvage the Russian warship the *Gangut*, which sank in the Gulf of Finland. Since then they have been modernised several times. The pontoons are equipped with large hydraulic jacks, the tall stands for which are placed over a long well running from fore to aft in the midship line of the pontoons. When the jacks are in use, simple nine-inch cables are eased under the ship to be salvaged and up through the shaft between the two halves of the pontoons. With this method, however, the wreck can only be raised until it reaches the bottom of the pontoons. To be able to carry out the salvage of the Vasa, it was considered appropriate to try from the very beginning to bring the ship up so high that they could begin pumping the water out while the Vasa was suspended in relative safety between the pontoons. To solve this and a number of other problems, the Neptune Company decided to move the jacks out to the sides of the pontoons. The displacement reserve of the pontoons was considered to be sufficient to manage the trimming needed to balance up the list. In round numbers, the Vasa's weight was estimated at this point to be 600 tons. Each of the pontoons were able to lift 1,200 tons.

The day after the press conference, the *Oden* and the *Frigg* were filled with water and lowered, after which the six-inch cables used for moving her in 1959 were linked together. They were still lying there under the ship. Once this was done, the water was pumped out of the pontoons and the Vasa raised slowly for about three metres. When the divers went down to check the situation, it turned out that the Vasa had slipped out of the grasp of the cables. The ship had to be returned to the sea bed and the divers to start dredging their way down along the sternpost to be able to insert another pair of cables from the stern. However, it turned out that this safety measure alone was not enough. To cover all eventualities, at an early stage, rubber lifting pontoons had been acquired with a total lifting force of twenty tons. These were also brought in astern as extra support.

A few days later, the all clear was given to start lifting again. The divers were now for the first time to have a chance of seeing what the bottom of the ship really looked like. They were probably perfectly aware that there were some holes in it,

**First on board the Vasa are Anders Franzén and Per Edvin Fälting
to receive tributes from the people.**

but was there any greater damage, perhaps impossible to repair? Nothing was known about that. From several points of view, the inspection of the bottom was exciting, nor was it entirely free of risk. Waves from the wash of careless seafarers would quite easily set the ship swaying – a movement that would crush the divers to death. Repeated navigational warnings were issued and every day the radio urged the greatest caution to all sea-going vessels. Two of the naval clearing divers were the first to slip down underneath the Vasa. Their first report sounded promising. She was looking fine. There were scarcely any marks at all on the huge keel from the cables that had carried the ship in 1959 on her eighteen-stage trip. The bottom planks were as hard as rock.

The sealing work continued, also the changing of cables. The old six-inch cables were to be replaced by thicker ones, to be linked to the lifting chains, the so-called Gall's chains, of the jacks. These look like gigantic bicycle chains.

Time passed. The day for the great lift had not yet been definitely decided on. It was a difficult decision, but it had to be taken. At last everything seemed to be going according to plan, and on April 14th, the time was considered ripe for the important decision. Monday, April 24th was to be the great day.

The coupling of the nine-inch cables to the Gall's chains went even faster than had been calculated, so on April 17th, the Vasa finally left the clay bottom of the harbour. Early in the morning, the fourteen jacks were manned – two men to each – and extremely carefully, centimetre by centimetre, the hydraulics hauled up the chain. The manometers on each jack were watched carefully. Nearly 220 tons were now resting on the port side jacks. That meant the Vasa still had a list. The total weight of the ship, according to the lastest calculations, had been reduced to about 400 tons, a pleasing reduction achieved by the energetic clearing work of the divers. A gun, a few tons of stone, a great many cubic metres of silt, dross and ash, as well as a number of pieces of sea-drenched oak weigh quite a bit. Keeping pace with the lifting, the pontoons had to be trimmed by counter-filling with water, so that they did not list too strongly towards the ship. The voyage from the bottom went well and towards evening, the Vasa was safely suspended with her upper parts a few metres below the surface.

Then the great day of resurrection arrived on April 24th. For the Neptune Company and the naval salvage team, it was one of a large number of working days, but also a historic day. At last they would be able to see the ship that had been invisible for 333 years – the ship that had been the object of so much effort, so much labour and so much discussion. It was brilliantly sunnny, a day filled with expectations, excitement and perhaps with a touch of anxiety in the air. Women naval auxillaries, warship crews, Vasa officials and many others began as early as at five in the morning to set off for Skeppsholmen to make the last preparations. About three hundred Swedish and foreign representatives of the media had requested to be allowed to be present at the raising to the surface. Nor was it long before they began to pour in to assure themselves a good place, to catch a few glimpses of morning-bright salvagers, find time for a special interview with Axel Hedberg, or at least try to save their reputations with a brief report and some pictures before the first edition went to press.

Motor-boats from the Navy and the Naval Defence Corps were ready to begin the day's shuttling the special guests. All round the salvage fleet, boats keeping order were circling to keep unauthorised sea traffic in check, flags fluttering on the salvage craft and every other ship in the harbour. A Vasa exhibition had also been arranged ashore.

The salvage fleet had quite suddenly been turned into an arena in a large watery stadium. Astern of the Vasa was the harbour's pontoon crane, the *Lodbrok*, a spacious and reliable stand for spectators. Its great crane construction provided excellent angles for cameras of every kind. The photographers also made the most of their acrobatic skills to an extent that it was a miracle no one fell into the water in the eagerness to get the picture of the day. Alongside the *Lodbrok* were two island steamers, and another had anchored to the fore of the Vasa.

There was a crowd of guests on board the *Sleipner*, State Councillors, admirals, generals, heads of industry, senior academics and museum officials.

The Navy's band was playing on the *Lodbrok* and in between commentaries on the situation were being given through loudspeakers. All available helicopters in the city had been hired by various newspapers and photographic agencies, so there was some reason to expect something of an air show above the Vasa. To avoid any accidents, it had even been considered necessary to establish traffic control by the Air Force on the *Belos*. The Neptune Company's staff were ready with their hydraulic jacks. The moment of breakthrough had arrived.

A few minutes before nine, the Vice-Chairman of the Wasa Commission climbed on to the beflagged platform on the *Sleipner* to welcome everyone. The Navy's band struck up a march and then the moment everyone had been waiting for came. It was three minutes past nine when the cubic foot of black seventeenth century oak appeared up out of the brown water, the remains of the badly shattered sterncastle first beginning to show itself. Endlessly slowly, the row of ribs of the bulwark stanchions began to rise out of the water. By ten o'clock the Vasa was emerging even more boldly. At about eleven, the fore began competing with the sterncastle. While the salvage men surely and safely handled the jacks, trimmed the pontoons and unhooked Gall's chains, jumping to orders from Hedberg, the Vasa rose by about 45 centimetres an hour. From up on the *Lodbrok* it was soon possible to make out the entire contour of the deck. On the foredeck appeared a pair of carved wooden knightheads. Through the sheaveholes in these knights ran some of the ropes once needed to manoeuvre the foremast sails and yards.

It was two o'clock or just after in the afternoon by the time the deckline appeared up on the surface. Anders Franzén and Per Edvin Fälting got ready to go on board and take possession of the ship. With applause from the great crowd, they both rowed a round of honour in a plastic dinghy across the deck of the Vasa, stepped aboard on to a deck beam in the stern, shook hands and offered a coin to »The Old One«.

From the public's point of view, the day was over. But the salvage team still had a few hours' work left for the next day's move in to shallower water.

PUMPMEN AND MUDSKIPPERS

ARLY in the morning the day after the lifting through the surface, the tug boats arrived. Towing cables were cast off and the entire armada was towed slowly about 200 metres closer to land. The whole procedure was carried out in about half an hour and the Vasa anchored with her fore four metres above the sea bed at a depth of ten metres, while her stern could just touch bottom at twelve metres.

The pump team and archaeologists were aching to make their contribution. But before the cleansing pumping could begin, the Vasa had to be raised another half a metre. The sun was hot and the conservation experts were looking anxiously at the wooden knights, the bulwark stanchions and deck beams. The most vulnerable parts had to be quickly covered with protective plastic, and also effective spraying with water had to be started as soon as possible to prevent all too quick drying out of the timbers.

Submergable pumps were all ready on the deck of the *Oden*, powerful gear, though despite their considerable capacity – ten tons a minute – they weighed no more than 500 kilos each.

The pumping was a fastidious element demanding great vigilence, and it also had to be synchronised with the lifting work. The water level inside the ship was never to be higher than outside. If that should happen, the Vasa would be exposed to abnormal strains in the form of pressure directed outwards. The iron rods that had been drawn in four places right through the ship might perhaps have prevented a disaster, but at this stage no one was taking any risks. As the Vasa began to rise, through trimming the lifting strength and speed of the pontoons had to be continuously regulated, so that the ship constantly had the support of the lifting cables.

Two pumps were lowered into their pumping shafts, one to the fore, the other astern, having previously been put in order by the divers. Soon 20,000 litres of water per minute were pouring out of the Vasa's hull.

Strangely enough, during the installation of the pumps, one of the Vasa's own wooden pumps had been found. This pumping house, once made watertight with pitch, was still watertight. The seventeenth century pump would have managed to pump out between 20 and 50 litres per minute, depending on the manning of the levers.

As soon as the pumping began, the divers again had to be quick. The Vasa was leaking badly through a great many invisible holes. With sawdust, tallow and rags, plugs and wedges, divers set about the leaks, which proved very difficult to localise. Gradually it was also found that one of the sealing pieces covering a gun-port had shiften position during the work with lifting cables. More water was pouring through that hole than the pumps could pump out, Towards the afternoon, however, the efforts of the divers were crowned with some success, the pumps began to gain ground and by the evening the foreship and sternship were almost two metres above the water level. The great beams carrying the upper deck were now well out of the water. Sixteen of them were still in their original places, while over the years twelve had been torn from their fastenings by ship anchors.

As the pumps sucked and the divers sealed, the archaeologists were preparing their contributions. The head archaologist, Per Lundström, mustered his small army consisting of ten students from the University of Stockholm, all of whom had had previous experience of archaeological excavations, ethnographical and art-history fieldwork. A quick glance down into the silt-covered hold of the Vasa was enough to see what awaited them all. But their wise leader had considered the worst scenario and his team was armed to the teeth – inoculated against tetanus, typhus, typhoid, paratyphus and other infectious diseases, clad from top to toe in rubber clothing and wearing protective helmets, they went to work in the sluggishly flowing, evil-smelling rotting sediment. The salvage leader was impatient and wanted to start a forced excavation astern as soon as possible. The ship was hanging heavily in the stern cables and had to be lightened.

The advantage the pumps had over the water pouring in grew greater. As the hours went by, more and more of the old ship's shape became visible. The working day of the archaeologists now amounted to at least twelve hours. The first day's harvest became all told two tons of deck beams, oak knees, indefinable pieces of timber, heavy pieces and light, all conveyed by the lifting crane for registration,

The gates to the Gustav V Dock are too narrow for the whole of the Vasa and the lifting pontoons. The Vasa had to float in the last bit on her own keel.

A box made of shavings belonging to a member of the crew and containing the remains of provisions brought with him is one of the many personal possessions found on board.

photographing and soaking. The leader's right hand man had set up his little head-quarters on a pair of pontoons moored astern of the Vasa, where there were ten or so bath tubs full of water into which the vulnerable finds were immediately put after registration. Larger pieces of the hull were wrapped in plastic and tarpaulins. All the objects had to be labelled with stainless steel number plates and the main data on them entered into special records of finds. It was considered necessary to register thoroughly just where in the ship the different finds had been made. Astern where Chief Ordnance Master Erik Jönsson and the commander of the ship, Söf-ring Hansson, had once had their living quarters, now looked like a gold-digger's camp. After the bulkiest and heaviest objects had been cleared away, the working method was changed. Muddy archaeologists worked with specially constructed washing troughs in which they rinsed and washed for dear life, and the stream of finds rapidly increased. Now and again the archaeologists were rewarded with some kind of rarity – a casket containing a couple of handsome pewter bottles, a distinc-tive sculpture, some angel musicians with clear traces of gilding on them, and so on.

The pumping went well, but as the water sank, it left behind huge quantities of silt. On the upper battery deck, the silt lay in half-metre thick layers. But on both the lower battery deck and the orlop deck, everything was buried under a metre-thick layer. The entire hold was filled with the same bubbling witch's brew, objects of varying kinds everywhere in the sediment. Before the work was completed, the main part of the sediment was to have passed through the archaeologists' pans.

While the salvage operation was at its height, the Vasa pontoon had been formal-ly launched in Gävle and was now expected in Stockholm. In the dry dock, the naval shipyard men had put in order a gravel bed on which the gigantic concrete box was to be placed. Inside the shipyard, they were preparing to receive the Vasa. It would not be long before the ship was also to be docked. Early in the morning of April 29th, the pontoon arrived at Beckholmen, where the shipyard men were impatiently waiting. With scarcely a metre's margin on each side, the pontoon was manoeuvered in over the gravel bed into the inner half of the dock. The dock gates were closed and the water pumped out. The keel blocks, on which the Vasa was to stand, were rigged and the support arrangements checked. After a few days, the pontoon could be filled with water, and then again the water pour into the dry dock. So now the future »museum floor« lay at the bottom of the dock. The inten-tion was that in time the Vasa would be docked down on to the pontoon.

On board the Vasa, archaeologists, salvage men and pumping experts were sweating. The ship was refusing to float up sufficiently. Her depth was still too great for the passage through the dock entrance. The depth at the entrance was about

When the Vasa capsized, part of the 120 tons of ballast ended up on the port side.

Remains of skeletons of 25 people were found during the salvaging. They have made interesting material for osteological research.

nine and a half metres and that ought perhaps to have been possible to manage in reasonable time. But what was worse, the Vasa had to be up on the almost four metre high pontoon, so was not to lie any deeper than around five and a half metres.

The unexpectedly large quantities of silt in the hold of the ship complicated their work. It became necessary to bring in special suction pumps into a special pump shaft in the middle of the ship. The Flygt pump chosen for this purpose had really been constructed to clear overgrown lakes. It sucked about eight tons of clay silt per minute out of the silt-filled hull. To protect finds that might lie hidden in the sediment at the very bottom by the keel, the suction funnel was fitted with a fine-meshed net. The battle against silt and water pouring in was fought fiercely and purposefully. Sometimes both enemies were victorious and the Vasa sank back a few feet. Sometimes the Vasa men got the upper hand and the rough oak sides rose yet another few inches. The battle swung to and fro for several days filled with tension.

In the way of seafarers, at this stage the salvagers never wholeheartedly dared speculate on successes not yet achieved. Fate is not challenged in all too optimistic terms by going in advance of events. Most questions on what would happen next were answered in vague terms and the answers always ended with definite reservations about unpredictable events. Anything can happen in the salvage trade. Captain Axel Hedberg and his men planned every step to be taken with great thoroughness, discussing what might happen at different stages and preparing appropriate counter-measures.

The lovely weather held. Day after day, the sun shone from a cloudless sky, the wind warm and gentle. Everyone was enjoying the lovely spring weather except the men on the Vasa, who, with rising anxiety, could see deck beams, railing supports and ship's sides beginning to dry out quickly in the bright sunlight. They had already covered the most vulnerable parts of the ship with plastic and spraying with water was continuous. But now the conservation experts wanted to have a real soaking through an effective sprinkling system that could keep the whole of the ship moist.

The archaeologists were having a truly troublesome time, sliding around in the evil-smelling mud, crawling on all fours through narrow holes, sweating in their tight-fitting rubber suits, tripping over hosepipes and fallen peices of the hull. They had to move ahead with great caution, for the layers of silt might be hiding a treacherous hole anywhere in the deck. To add to it all, they were now having to work beneath the endless stream of water from the sprinklers. But the heap of excavated finds grew swiftly under the protective tarpaulin at the collecting station

Fälting tasting the contents of one of the many preserving vessels in the form of barrels, kegs and boxes found on board.

Only one gold object was found in the Vasa, a signet ring, which unfortunately lacked the stone that would have identified its owner.

and in long rows of baths full of water.

The pump men now had the situation under control. The pumps were running day and night and pitch-black water mixed with silt was pouring in huge quantities along the ship's sides. The moment also came when the Vasa was afloat, when for the very first time she moved in the swell caused by a passing motor-boat. It was an unaccustomed, akward movement, but nevertheless a much longed-for sign of life. The Vasa was now soon to be taken into dry dock. But she was not going to submit to the salvagers' efforts that easily. She was still lying too deeply for them to place her on to the pontoon. It was not only sediment and water weighing down the ship. The soaked oak of the ship's sides and the huge beams were also heavy. They could not get the Vasa to float up sufficiently with nothing but help from the pumps. What was needed was radical and swift measures. The salvage vessels could not stay there for ever, as they were needed for other assignments. Could the archaeologists step up their work even more? No, and again, no. They were already toiling away for over twelve hours a day. From a scientific point of view, it would also be straight reprehensible to hasten the excavation of this utterly unique find of a ship.

Instead of docking the Vasa directly on to the pontoon, they now had to do the docking in two stages. Fortunately, the dry dock was so large that the Vasa could be placed astern of the big pontoon. The archaeologists could work there more efficiently and in calmer conditions than right out in the middle of Stockholm harbour. The new line of action was quickly decided on. Now it was a question of towing the Vasa into dry dock as soon as possible. »We start at twelve o'clock tomorrow,« declared Captain Hedberg.

There were no more than twenty hours left before this historical little journey was to begin on Thursday, May 4th, a few days earlier than had originally been planned. The order also gave rise to intense activity on all fronts. First and foremost, the Vasa's list had to be righted as best it could. That was to be done with the help of ten tons of ballast placed to starboard on the upper battery deck. In all haste, tugboats and lifting cranes were commandeered. The pontoon crane *Lodbrok* was also needed for moving the great mooring buoys. Twelve o'clock came, but no sign of the *Lodbrok*. The shores along the fairway were already black with people wanting to see the Vasa making her last journey on her own keel.

Captain Hedberg was looking impatiently out for *Lodbrok's* tall crane construction, the tugboats ready, the mooring had been simplified and everything was ready for departure. At last the familiar contour of the crane hove into sight above Beckholmen. By the time the message of the the Vasa's docking had come, the pontoon crane had already been promised eleswhere to place a 6,000 horse-power diesel engine into a merchant ship and the work had been slightly delayed. Just before one o'clock, however, the salvage armada began to move. The weather was ideal, with sun and no wind. Slowly, the tugboats began pulling, at first a slow swing round with the entire salvage fleet – a difficult manoeuvre in that narrow fairway. Then at last the Vasa's bulging forebody was pointing in the right direction and at a speed of two knots, on a course for Beckholmen dock.

Just before two o'clock, Captain Hedberg was able to start the next swing round on exactly the same spot where the Vasa had sunk in 1628. The *Lodbrok* had already placed out the two buoys the salvage ships needed to take direction in towards the entrance of the dock. Now remained the last and most exciting element. As the lifting pontoons could not go with the ship through the entrance of the dock, the cables had to be cast off and the Vasa had to manage the last bit on her own. For a moment things looked threatening when one of the stern cables caught somewhere on the bottom of the Vasa, but a pair of divers settled that. The lifting cable from the dock's great crane was linked to the Vasa. Freed from all the lifting pontoons and salvage ships, the old ship glided on her own keel with a slight list into the safe haven of the dock at about five o'clock. A relieved Captain Hedberg lit a cigar and gave the V-sign. His part of the work was over. The staff of the naval shipyard were now to take over.

Parts of one huge anchor cable remained, saved by two barrels of pitch breaking during the disaster and soaking the cordage. The rest were a mass of dissolved fibres.

**The Vasa is now in safe keeping after the completed salvaging,
propped on the keel blocks on her concrete pontoon,
which is to carry her to the provisional Wasa Shipyard
and finally to the permanent Vasa Museum.**

DRY DOCK AT LAST

ONCE the dock gates were closed on the Vasa, a new stage began in the life of the ship, now that the risk of the Vasa sinking again no longer existed. Instead, other factors were lying in wait. No one really knew how the hull would react to sunlight and heat. Nor did anyone know with any certainty what might happen when the ship was in dry dock. Would she stand these new strains? How should they best support the ship to prevent cracks forming and subsidence in the hull? Would she tolerate being dried out with all her ballast still inside? How much ballast was there inside her? How quickly could it be got out? The problems again piled up for the Vasa team.

Nor were they given any peace and quiet to solve their problems. According to the plan, the Vasa was to remain in dock until June 17th, i.e. roughly six weeks, but after that she had to leave for the icebreakers to be made ready for the coming winter. To be able to keep to schedule, the Vasa team still had to go on working at high pressure. Much work remained before the Vasa, floating on her big concrete pontoon, could be towed to the planned mooring place in Djurgården.

The first days in dock were exciting. Slowly and cautiously, the water was pumped out, while the Vasa was carefully shored up all along her sides and from below. More and more of the ship became visible. The 333 years on the sea bed had naturally not gone by without trace. But they did not appear to have caused much wear to the solid oak hull. The main deck was ripped up, but the remaining deck beams provided a good idea of what it had once looked like. Timber ribs and bulwark stanchions rose above the deck line, some whole, others broken off. The high sterncastle where the officers had had their quarters had collapsed completely.

The Vasa's hull was impressive. The spacious forebody gave an impression of solid strength, but the wide bow was also evidence that the Vasa was no swift sailing ship, her ability to manoeuver probably not of the best. The black sides of the ship, glistening with moisture, rose out of the depths of Beckholmen dock like the walls of a building. Through the double gun-port rows of square holes, a seventeenth century atmosphere streamed out towards visitors. The water line was about four foot below the lower row of gun-ports. High rigging, huge superstructures, heavy guns and a richly carved ornamentation placed high up, made all ships of the time unstable. From the stern, the ship's underwater body looked almost graceful. The sprawling remains of the sterncastle ended almost thirteen metres above the keel. The rudder was over ten metres high and weighed almost three tons. Everything belonging to the Vasa is large, massive and heavy. Over a thousand gigantic mature oaks must have been used to build her.

Gradually it also became possible to allow the general public to see the ship at close quarters. People in their thousands poured in. Seldom has an audience been more interested, impressed and eager to know more. They stood on the edge of the dock, arguing, looking and marvelling.

The days went by. The archaeologists were working at full tilt, the crane on the quay lifting basket after basket of new finds, small and large pieces of timber, seamen's chests, pieces of rigging, carvings, cannon-balls and much else. The containers for soaking them were insufficient to receive the stream of finds, so new ones were hastily made for the temporary preservation of the many precious items.

On Sweden's Flag Day, June 6th, the Vasa received a special tribute when the Vasa team accepted from the hand of the king a replica of the flag the ship should once had flown. The new flag was 6.5 metres long and 4 metres high. The colours are considerably richer than on present day Swedish flags: dark indigo blue and an orangey yellow. The colours had been found on an old Swedish flag preserved in Amsterdam, a flag captured by the Dutch at the battle of Öresund in 1658 and the oldest known preserved Swedish royal ensign.

The now all-overshadowing problem was to get the Vasa up on to the pontoon. The ballast was inaccessible down in the hold. Despite their intensive efforts, the archaeologists had not succeeded in extracting sufficient of the enormous layers of silt each day. The Vasa was still too heavy and would lie too deep when the dock was again filled with water. The level of water had in addition been abnormally low over recent days. Something had to be done if the time schedule were not to fall apart completely. Captain Hedberg, who had recently completed his part of the operation, was recalled. It was necessary to do a salvage operation in miniature, to

**Once in dock, help from the cylindrical pontoons was necessary
to get the Vasa up on to the concrete pontoon on which she was to stand in future.**

lift the Vasa with the help of smaller pontoons that would go alongside the ship inside the dock.

The Neptune Company's men were once again to be seen round the Vasa. Four cylindrical pontoons with a lifting power of nearly 100 tons each were connected and everything made ready for a very last lifting. The water level, however, was still low, and not even with the help of the pontoons could she be got into place. But then suddenly one evening, the water rose rapidly. At the same time the weather forecasts gave a warning that it would soon lower again. Lightning action was required. The dock was filled with water and soon the Vasa was floating again. Slowly and cautiously, she was drawn forward over her future museum floor. It became a precision job. The margins were very small and the ship floated in over the keel blocks with a centimetre to spare astern. Everyone drew a sigh of relief once she was at last in place.

The difficulties getting the Vasa up on to the pontoon had also indicated that the ship was considerably heavier than had at first been estimated. So now it was a matter of lightening the hull of sediment and ballast as quickly as possible. To get rid of the viscous silt, they were forced to use a suction-spool method, which entailed cautiously pumping in quite large quantities of water into the hull. The water dissolved the mud down in the hold into a thin gruel which slowly but surely could then be pumped out. As soon as the layers of sediment had been sufficiently reduced, the problem of the ballast could be solved with the use of a conveyor belt.

The ballast had been calculated to weigh about 400 tons, so it was a surprise when it was established that the Vasa had no more than 120 tons of stones in her hold, far too little for a ship of her size. Sucking out the silt, excavating and removing the ballast took some time, and in the race with time, the Vasa team lost. The parade planned to take place in Stockholm waters on June 17th 1961 in connection with the towing to the Wasa Shipyard, the provisional museum, had to be cancelled. Instead, there was a mass invasion of visitors to the Beckholmen dock, where the Vasa gradually acquired the company of the ice-breaker the *Ymer*. Almost 20,000 people went on a pilgrimage to see the Vasa the weekend when at a formal ceremony the man-of-war's own ensign was hoisted for the first time.

The work took its time. Days went by and the Vasa was still in dock. Not until July 26th, quite without fuss, did she leave the dock, forty days later than had at first been calculated.

But where was the Vasa to go after her period in dock? How could she be made accessible to the general public? It was a problem that had had to be solved alongside that of salvaging and excavation. After a great many discussions, it was gradually decided on an area in Djurgården just by Liljevalch's art hall and immediately opposite Skeppsholmen. It would be possible to tow the pontoon right up against the land there. An area of land judged to be sufficiently large to contain the shore installations required to give the ship an appropriate framework was also available. The planning of what is called the Wasa Shipyard began as early as in December 1960. A great many intricate problems of a technical-constructional and architectonic kind were involved in the work. For technical conservation reasons, the Vasa had to be protected by a superstructure in which it would be possible to control both moisture and temperature. This had to be ready before autumn came with night frosts. The building of the framework of the building which was to house the Vasa until 1989 had already been begun during the docking period. The shape of the superstructure was dictated by the shape of the ship. The 56 metre long side walls were inclined inwards and the roof line followed the ship's sheer with its strongly marked sternposts.

The Wasa Shipyard was opened to the public at the end of 1961, but no ceremonial inauguration took place until February 16th, 1962. The whole arrangement was considered to be provisional. After ten years, when the »wet« part of the conservation work was premised to be complete, it was to be replaced by a permanent museum building worthy of one of Sweden's leading tourist attractions.

The lower gun-deck of the Vasa, an environment from the distant past to stir the imagination. The gun carriages are in place by the gun-ports. To the fore is a glimpse of the bitts to which the anchor cable was fastened when at anchor.

Uniforms did not yet exist in the Navy. Each man brought his own clothes on board. The usual clothing was a linen shirt, breeches and a short homespun jacket, sewn stockings and leather shoes.

FINDS TELL THEIR STORY

WHILE the technicians were wracking their brains to deal with the docking of the ship, the move up on to the pontoon, the shoring etc., with undiminshed energy, the archaeologists continued their scientific offensive to reconquer a re-born seventeenth century society. The register of finds grew rapidly. A rare mixture of apparently worthless bits of wood, interesting useful objects and imaginative carvings had been brought up into the light of day. The experts rubbed their hands with delight when faced with this wealth of well-preserved finds. As good as daily, marine scholars, ethnologists and art historians had something new to ponder over. The heaps of bits of puzzle grew.

It is inconceivable in this context to account for all the objects the archaeologists came over. It has already been established that the Vasa was a splendid ship with all her painted and gilded carvings. But what was it like behind this showpiece façade? Had conditions on board really corresponded to the magnificence of the carvings? No, far from it. Life for seamen of the day was both plain and hard. Pay was bad, the food wretched, clothes simple, and the many finds have clarified various aspects of life on board. But important documents touching on the origins and manning of the ship have been lost, including, for instance, the crew list which according to the king's instruction of April 28th, 1628, had been drawn up for the Vasa. The list of survivors of the disaster is also missing, as are some of the pages from the records of the hearing after the capsizing, as well as certain bills from the shipyard. The latter were once confiscated at the enquiry begun on the orders of the king in the autumn of 1628 into the entrepeneurs who had long run the shipyard and other tasks for the Navy. So here was a great deal of work for interested archivists.

Naturally it was also important to attempt to clarify which other equipment of importance ought justifiably to have been found among what was found on board. Vulnerable objects had been destroyed under the water and others had been salvaged by bold seventeenth century divers. Perhaps forgotten letters and other documents would eventually help to spread more light on the harsh life at sea in the fleet of warships of Sweden's great days of glory. Many very interesting finds from the more well-equipped ship the *Kronan*, lost in 1676, were a valuable complement.

The remains of some of the unfortunates who went down with the Vasa were found crushed under gun-carriages or lying in the mud. Next to a gun-carriage was a complete skeleton, still on it parts of his clothing and a pair of well-preserved leather shoes. During the clearing of the sea bed area round the hollow in which the Vasa had lain, the remains of yet another number of victims were found. Several of the skeletons had clear traces of earlier accidents, arms and legs broken after severe blows. In some cases, tooth enamel testifies to periods of undernourishment, and the surfaces of molars are often quite level. The flour used for baking bread had clearly often contained some grit from the mill wheels. Some wretches bore clear testimonies of virulent pus-formation in their jaws. Preserved parts of skeletons and skulls with grinning rows of teeth have provided archaeologists, osteologists and dental surgeons with interesting material to examine.

It is known that the seamen came from coastal parishes and towns. Out of ten citizens, one good and capable seaman was to be taken from the towns into the service of the Crown. During the 1620's it was also decided that conscripts with families and belongings were to move to Stockholm and remain there in future. In 1623, the king decided that four companies of 400 seamen were to be set up. They became the Nyland, Åboland, Åland and Värmdö Companies.

It was prescribed that the men conscripted should be between 18 and 40, healthy and fit to bear arms, and it was particularly pointed out that the lines were not, as before, to be filled with »cripples and disabled men«. Men suffering from infectious diseases, as well as criminals were not to be taken out. Vagrants, on the other hand, were conscripted without hesitation. It is clear that peasants and citizens did not voluntarily let their best men go. Nor was life on warships of the day anything men voluntarily allowed themselves to be conscripted into. Some of the men are known from the records of the hearing. It would be interesting to be able to make even a superficial acquaintance with the rest of the Vasa's crew.

To return to the emptied gun-decks, which as early as at the beginning of the 1960's had been cleared of their equipment, the seventeenth century atmosphere nevertheless was still tangible down in the Vasa's interior. Traces from carpenters'

The case of a table clock of which the dial and works were unfortunately missing, copper coins, a gold ring, a clay pipe and a bronze candlestick.

Handsome beer flasks turned on a lathe out of curly-grained birchwood.

axes can be seen in the deck planking and knees. Gun-carriages, plundered of their guns by seventeenth century divers, were still there in their original places, on some their lashings also in place. So Erik Jönsson, the chief ordnance master, had told the truth at the trial when he had testified that all the Vasa's guns had been well secured, so had had no part in the disaster that had occurred.

Seamen and their familes had shared rooms on the gun-decks during the short trip to disaster. In wartime, about 300 soldiers and almost 140 seamen were to share the living space between the guns, perhaps for month-long expeditions. Forty years or so were to pass before naval crews were given hammocks to sleep in. In a circular dated 1675, the staff of the Admiralty writes to the company commanders to say: »and as is known, the cause of sickness among seamen during the last expedition has been that they had no other clothing except what they wore daily, captains should in the best way and manner prevail upon every unit to give every man as much coarse cloth from which he can make a hammock and a cover, which solely for this time be imposed on him as an extra task.«

The officers did indeed live separately from the crew in different spaces in the high sterncastle, though even there comfort was not very noticeable. Restoration work has shown that there were a few fixed folding bunks in the officers' quarters.

The Crown was very mean with personal equipment. Uniforms did not exist, each man had to dress according to taste and assets. Both officers and men were said to have long received part of their pay in the form of some kind of cloth. In a 1621 pay regulation, however, it was decided that cloth was no longer to be paid as an emolument and the men were to have money instead. This regulation was not popular and was abolished a few years later. What man bought cloth when he needed food? In 1634, it was decided that the Crown should provide clothing for the men while they were in service. What it was like for the Vasa men is not known. However, one thing that is certain is that the men's personal equipment was extremely meagre. The lack of finds in this field speaks loudly of this as well. No extra clothing for cold nights on deck and no wet-weather clothing. Nor are such luxury items mentioned in the orders and instructions of the day. In wartime, when expeditions at sea often began early in the spring and sometimes went on until late in the year, the cold, rain and snow could make service as good as unbearable. There was nowhere to dry their wet homepsun clothing in the unheated ships. Frostbite was a common ailment often leading to amputation of an arm or a leg. In both 1627 and in 1628, the last units of the Swedish blockade squadrons lay anchored off Danzig well into December.

Diseases often ravaged the ships. The lack of drinking water, crowded conditions

**At the bottom ot the hold fore of the main mast was the galley,
consisting of a brick floor and two tranverse-ship brick walls,
the space open at the sides. The food was cooked over an open fire.**

In the officers' quarters in the sterncastle were found the more costly
table objects, including a tankard, flask, butterbox and plates made of pewter,
a Dutch earthenware plate, ceramic jars, one with a pewter lid,
an elegant bronze chafing dish, a glass bottle and a tall octagonal wine glass.

A large quantity of ceramic objects had survived the centuries very well,
among them bowls, three-legged pans, drinking cups and cans.
Here is also a flask which could be carried on a strap.

**In a round box with a house-mark carved into the lid
were the possessions of one of the crew, a wooden spoon,
a bone comb, a sewing ring and a knife handle.
Also material for mending shoes – thread, wax and tacks.**

and poor ventilation all contributed to spread them. Most feared of all were dysentery and scurvy. Sometimes it could be that sickness put out of action over half the seamen in a whole squadron.

A great many interesting finds were made on the battery decks. Apart from gun-carriages, there were accessories for the guns – ramrods, gunpowder kegs, wedges and handspikes. But what perhaps captivated the archaeologists most of all were the personal items scattered everywhere in the foot-deep silt, necessities of a simpler kind – eating utensils and food vessels. There were pewter and wooden plates, ceramic bowls, clay cups, cans and jars, wooden spoons and so on. Clay goods and wooden objects were the seamen's. The expensive pewter was found in the stern-castle where the officers had their quarters, including some fine, elegantly shaped pewter flasks and a lovely pewter chamber pot. Among the luxury articles were a small table chafing dish to keep food warm, a tap, the top in the shape of a cockerel, a pocket sundial made of wood and a table clock. Among the many small personal belongings were, for instance, a fine comb, buttons, hooks and eyes, a breast-pin and a box with a lock of hair in it. The only gold object found on board was a signet ring, unfortunately with no stone in it that might have revealed something of its owner.

Several seamen's chests were found on board and opening the first one was a festive moment for a reverential little group who had the advantage of witnessing this remarkable event. On top inside the oak chest that had been packed over 300 years ago was a well-preserved felt hat. Next to it was a chip-box that turned out to contain a sewing ring, wax, a comb, the remains of a knife with a mother-of-pearl handle, a skein of wool and some pieces of cloth. Under the hat was a keg measuring about two litres of liquor. There was also a pair of slippers, a pair of shoes and a wooden last used for orders for or for making new shoes. Shoe-lasts, pegs and pieces of leather were found in several chests and finds. Salt water and the work on deck or aloft were hard on footwear. At the bottom of the chest was a pair of well-preserved gloves made of hide and a money-purse of coins. The lock on the chest had rusted away and its contents were soaked in mud. Fragments of textiles were found in the sludge at the bottom. On the chip-box was a perfectly visible owner's mark.

Over 4,000 coins have been found in various parts of the ship. Of these, 55 were silver, the rest copper coins. Sweden had copper standard coinage and to speed up the pace of minting coins, had begun making what were called cuttings. They were square coins, made from long strips of copper, then stamped and cut into squares, hence the name. The majority of the coins found on board were cuttings of that

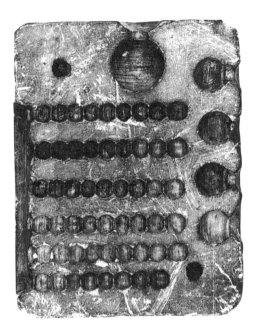
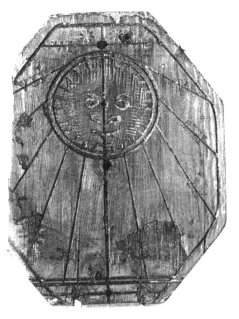

**Included in the odd finds is a mould for lead bullets
and the lid of a pocket sundial made of wood.
The handsome pewter chamber pot belonged to one of the officers on board.**

A large number of copper coins was found on board,
largely square coins, so-called cuttings.

Some of the officers had probably had this backgammon game
with them on board. It was found in the hold farthest astern
and is complete with counters and two small dice.

In a tool-chest was found the ship's carpenter's equipment.
Here, as elsewhere in the ship, the wrought iron had rusted away,
but all the wooden handles remained.

kind. The much discussed ship's money-chest, however, has been searched for in vain.

One of the pewter flasks found contained almost a litre of a rum-like drink of 33% alcohol strength, the aroma still good and rich. The butter found in a box and which the head diver Fälting in an unguarded moment tasted had not survived so well. Not only did it taste unpleasant, but also Fälting appeared the next day with a fierce rash round his mouth, although he was otherwise quite well.

Drinking vessels made of pewter, wood and clay are noticeably numerous and also the various beer kegs were found among the objects retrieved. Beer was an important ingredient of seventeenth century diet on board as much as ashore. The rations of beer of the day were large. But plenty of drink was no doubt necessary to wash down the salt, dry and often rancid food provided on board.

According to the 1535 Swedish maritime law, a barrel or about 125 litres of beer per day was allotted for 40 men. But three litres of beer per man per day was considered insufficient, and in 1559 the ration was increased to a barrel per 30 men. By the mid-seventeenth century it was considered a seaman should have at least three tankards (4 litres) a day at sea. The year the Vasa sank, King Gustav II Adolf prescribed that the Navy was to be supplied with bread and beer, »so that the men shall have their meagre sustenance and not need to drink the salt water that is the cause of so many in past years being lost to sickness and death, His Majesty and the Realm, to great damage and human loss« In this context it is worth mentioning that the king was well aware that beer was important to counteract scurvy, a sickness easily acquired at sea considering the food on offer. Beer was of three qualities, master-beer for officers and captains, bailiff-beer for shipmasters and helmsmen, and ship's-beer for the ordinary seamen. It can also be mentioned here that the Swedish Navy at this time consumed about 500,000 litres of beer per annum, with goodwill, for hungry or sick soldiers and seamen did not fight very well. But the stowage space on board was very limited and insufficient for provisions for any length of time. Should the supply of provisions from ashore during wartime become poor, then so did the beer-drinking situation. The brackish waters of the Baltic had to serve as a poor alternative, often generating sickness.

Once the battery decks had been cleared by the summer of 1961, the work continued down in the hold of the ship, a matter primarily of freeing the ballast so that it could be removed. The ship's anchor hawsers were found there, all in all, 400 metres long with a diameter of 15 centimetres. Dry, they were calculated to weigh almost two and half tons, though unfortunately the cordage was in a very bad state. However, the contents of some tar barrels that had broken in the disaster had fortunately overflowed on to a part of the anchor hawser and preserved bits of it.

Various barrels containing cattle and pig bones were found in the storage space. In barrels which had held salted-down Baltic herrings, the bones were still there like a thick-piled rya rug on the bottom. For a change of diet from salt and dried food, the crew went fishing wherever they could, and this can be verified by fishing lines, net sinkers and floats found on board.

Six kegs of musket shot and a large number of 24-pounder cannon balls for the main artillery were found, as well as the other kind of ammunition for the guns, barshot, pike shot and chain shot. An interesting find was the carpenter's »work-tray« or tool-box, which contained articles such as a wooden drill handle, an axe handle, braces and planes, knife handles, whetstones and also a fishing-line reel. Like all wrought iron on board, the metal parts of the tools had rusted away, but the handles showed what tools the chest had contained. The carpenter's bench was also found.

The ship's galley was farthest down in the ship, immediately fore of the foot of the main mast. It consisted of a square space (2.2 × 2.75 metres) with a brick floor, a hearth resting on a clay bed. The space was open at the sides, but had brick walls fore and aft. The food was cooked on an open fire in a large cauldron hung on an iron rail between the brick walls. The pan held 180 litres, and when salvaged was found thrown over to the port side among the ballast stones, where it had landed when the Vasa heeled over to port and sank.

There were several pumps on board, one just fore of the steerage and consisting of an eight metre long hollowed-out alder trunk. So that the pump pipe should not dry and crack, the bark had been left on the trunk, and it is still there today. The other pump in the ship's centre line was placed astern of the main mast. It was of the double-action type and had pump pipes of lead. There was also another pump mid-ships on each side, also with lead pipes.

From April 25th to September 29th, the archaeologists worked at emptying the Vasa of her riches. During that period alone, 14,000 numbered finds were registered. In reality this means a larger number of individual finds, as a sealed find of coins, for instance, would be registered under one and the same number. During the continued diving work on the Vasa disaster site from 1963 to 1967, about 4,000 more objects were also found, among them the main part of the Vasa's sculptures. The total of numbered finds altogether comes to about 25,000.

»... openly board and do your best to unman and subdue the enemy's ship ...«
Oil painting by Adolf Bock, 1951.

TESTIMONY OF REALITY

I N 1628, yet another Swedish squadron lay at anchor off Danzig. The blockade had to continue despite the ignominious end of the previous year. Sailing home to Stockholm in November 1627, the Swedish squadron had found itself far too scattered and this had been smartly exploited by the Polish Admiral Dickman for an attack. The outcome was highly unfortunate for the Swedes. Their admiral, Nils Stiernsköld was killed, and his squadron ship the *Tigern* [the Tiger] struck colours. After further losses – among them the *Solen* [the Sun] which blew up – the Swedish squadron was forced to retreat from the battle.

The following year, in July 1628, Stiernsköld's remains were brought back to the capital with honours. The Vasa was then clearly complete and lying in Stockholm harbour, where together with *Stora Kronan* [Great Crown] she was ordered to salute the homecoming warrior's mortal remains. The notice of this can be found in the ordnance accounts: »Up at New Whassan delivered on July 5 Gunpowder to Fire when the blessed Stiernskiöld's corpse is carried through Strömmen July 5...«

On September 10th, 1628, to the day a month after the Vasa disaster, as duty admiral, Henrik Fleming issued an instruction to the fleet anchored at Danzig: »what now every man shall know what there to do«. The instruction is given on board the admiral's ship *Tre Kronor* [Three Crowns]. There were seven more ships in the squadron. In the first squadron, apart from the admiral's ship, was also the *Apollo*. In the second were the *Andromeda*, *Enhörningen* [the Unicorn], the *Månan* [the Moon] and the *Oraniebom*. The third squadron consisted of the *Sankt Jacob* [the St Jacob] and the *Delfin* [the Dolphin].

The instruction is a telling document, its curt form providing a tangible experience of the way war at sea was prepared and fought, what expectations the officers had of the men and what achievements were demanded of them. But it also contains a clear insight into the horrors of battle and awareness that it may be difficult to drive people to resist and function despite them.

At first come general regulations on how each captain or lieutenant is to ensure that his ship is correctly ballasted and »comfortable to sail, that it obeys the rudder and tacks well when one luffs and turns...« and how each and every man was to observe his situation in relation to his own and the enemy's ships in battle, so that he is not driven towards land or hinders his own by his manoeuvres.

Then the guns, the most important means of battle: »Every captain or lieutenant on his ship shall look to his pieces that they stand well in their ports and that all their accessories, with wheels, cordage, slings, crowbars, handspikes and ramrods etc. are in order and made ready. And that in time certain pieces are distributed to each gunner, over which he shall supervise, load and fire.« Each gunner shall in his turn have the help of his subordinates and soldiers detailed to each gun.

At every piece, they shall prepare themselves for battle. »Also for every piece shall be put in order 10 or 12 cartridges, which with caution should be filled as much as the pieces can tolerate and with consideration of the strength of the gunpowder. So shall the cannon balls of all kinds also lie to hands together with the waddings, so that during the actual work he does not have to run to and fro from the work, and perhaps take with him the wrong shot and wadding. And in that way hinder each other in the firing and loading.«

Fire on board was the greatest terror. The ships were highly inflammable with all their tarred timbers, sails and – not least – the gunpowder involved. If the fire took hold, the ship was irretrievably lost. Many were the ships lost from fire, whether through carelessness and their own fault or in battle with the enemy. A feared weapon were the tarred wreaths of fire and incendiary bombs thrown on board opponents' ships. So it was natural that Fleming should emphasize in his instruction the importance of doing everything to prevent fire on board.

»Ships shall with industry, as battle ensues, be wetted both outside and in, and between every pair of pieces a tub of water be placed, with which the pieces can be quenched. Similarly one shall with leather pails with skill and swiftness wet its sails, and always have the pail to hand to put out fire wherever, if, God forbid, it should break out. And a good number of sponges shall be in store, with which to clean pieces or wet the deck, under and over the pieces. And that the ship's sergeant is instructed with the other land sergeant always to have supervision of

**Most of the artillery ammunition consisted of round cannon balls.
But there was also special ammunition, for instance, chainshots and barshots,
which were primarily to wreck the rigging and sails of enemy ships.**

the fire. As the others are at their work, some also must be ordered to their help, which always must have good supervision that applies to fire both on upper and lower decks. And the scuppers shall be closed both up and down so that the water stands half a hand high on deck.

»So shall hides in the ship's stores be wetted and thrown into the pails together with salt, so that the hides can thus draw the salt to them and thus can dampen and extinguish any firework and fire the enemy has managed to throw on board the ship. ....

»Army officers shall place as many musketeers that are needed in every place where they can best damage the enemy, though careful not to stand too close together, so that they set fire to each other's bandoliers.«

In battle, it was primarily a matter of attempting to fire at enemy ships and sink them. But as the enemy must be presumed to have the same aim, Fleming instructs in the following way how to prepare for such a fatality that the ship is hit at the water line. »Carpenters shall have ready plugs and sheet-lead with nails, so should a shot below water occur, the leak can quickly be plugged. Inside shall also be good space along the ship's sides so that leaks can quickly soon be found, and plugged, using wool and tarred cloth, as grain bags, otherwise useful and good, at this time are not in store.«

Faced with battle, other preparations were also to be made.

»So shall also axes, boarding axes and sledgehammers be to hands to save his own and damage the enemy's ship and its rigging, wherever they happen to meet, and men should know how to use them on orders of the captain and shipmaster. In addition they shall have half pikes and a number of good boarding axes to hands beforehand ready for the soldiers' needs when they are to board the enemy's ship. Also shall they be used for good defence if the enemy should board, and together with exploding of stone-chests and firing of guns and muskets he shall then with axe blows and thrusts be driven from our ship again.

»And for the young men, both land and sea folk, to be even rougher and braver when they go into battle with the enemy, then one shall give them a pair of barrels of beer of the best kind to drink. For this I have ordered that 2 barrels shall be in store on every ship, and so shall they be exhorted to bravery and reminded of their fidelity to service, which they owe to God, the King and the Swedish realm to show to death and manfully remember.«

One of the Vasa's three preserved 24-pounders. They were decorated with the national coat-of-arms and the King's initials, but were badly cleaned and burnished after casting.

An undated drawing by Willem van de Velde the Elder is an interesting confirmation that the ship's guns could be loaded outboard. In the one case the loader is sitting astride the barrel, as he inserts the loading rod or the ramrod into the bore.

When the battle begins, the captain together with the shipmaster are to be up on deck to be responsible for the ship's manoeuvres, so that they are in the best position in relation to the enemy. The lieutenant is to be responsible for the ship's guns. It is also his task to make sure the men ordered to each gun during battle stay at their posts until another order comes.

> »Up in the tops shall be arranged 2 to 3 healthy and good men practised in throwing spears, burning tarred wreaths and grenades. They shall be ordered to throw them carefully into the enemy's ships and sails, and where they see the most people standing, they shall throw in the grenades into their ship. They shall also have with them loaded firearms and half pikes and axes to shoot, slash and hack those of the enemy who when boarding wish to climb and take down our flag.«

Going into battle was a frightening experience for most men on board. It depended on the courage and judgement of the officers whether the battle-morale could be kept up. So in the instructions, the ship's lieutenant was urged to exhort the men to bravery and also make quite certain no one ran away to hide. In several contexts it was pointed out that the men on board were young, clearly with little experience of what was awaiting them.

> »And when one of our people at God's will is shot to death, one shall soon throw his body aside and cover it with old sailcloth, if one does not have the chance to throw him down into the hold on the ballast. This so that he is not in the way of the others and that they at the sight of the dead shall be afraid and timid, for they are young folk.
> »So the officers shall urge them and strengthen their courage to avenge the deaths of their brothers-in-arms.
> »Those who are wounded shall be soon taken to the galley to the ship's barber to be bandaged. But one must ensure that many healthy men do not while pretending to be wounded leave and stay away from their labours.
> »The ship's lieutenant shall also urge men to bravery and with seriousness hinder all from hiding or keeping away. Just as also shall folk be exchanged, so that they who have used up their powder shall soon be sent down to the cabin to have their bandoliers filled again with gunpowder that their sergeant carefully gives to them. Men who are to relieve them shall hastily be driven up to their places with filled bandoliers.«

In an intersection model in the Vasa Museum,
activities on board can be studied – cooking the food in the galley,
rolling barrels, men working the capstan
and the wounded being cared for in the sick-bay.

If things were to go so badly that their own ship was so fiercely attacked that all the officers on board were killed, Fleming hopes that there was »an honest Swede and faithful man« who would set fire to the gunpowder store and blow the ship to pieces. Thus it would prevent the ship from falling into the enemy's hands. That was what had happened the previous year off Danzig.

But that was not what was to be the first consideration. No, instead it was a matter of doing the very best a man could do in battle.

»And when it comes to battle, no man shall shoot, either with guns or muskets, with less than that he has been ordered to by the ship's officers, and he is so close that he cannot miss the shot. And that must not happen hastily without aiming, at which our own as well as the enemy can be damaged, from which the enemy will take courage and our own be defeated. Instead shall each man give himself time with care with the guns, so that especially when he is fighting with the enemy, then not damage our own ship when he really means to damage the enemy.

»If he senses that the enemy has many men on his ship, every man shall do his best to force the enemy with guns and shoot everywhere he senses that most men are, at which he shall use pikeshots, chainshots and cross shots to damage his sail and cordage in his ship. When he comes close to the enemy's ship, he loads guns with linen sacks filled with musket shots and bar shots and shoots along the enemy deck... And when he senses terror has been afflicted on the enemy he shall bravely board according to position and opportunity with boarding axes and half pikes and do his best to take over and man the enemy's ship. But if he does not see any possibility of boarding, then he shall instead manoeuvre as close to the enemy as possible and keep firing at the waterline until inreparable damage has been done to him.«

Any man giving in in battle can only expect death. But he who keeps himself well can expect a reward. »Every captain, lieutenant, shipmaster or soldier, just as the land captains and his officers and men who in this prescribed for them, industriously, faithfully and manly in his deeds before others show his service to manliness – to him I say, that for our most gracious of kings I shall promote and help to a good reward. And should he have received some incurable injury or has lost his life, I shall with the greatest energies (in so far as God spares me my life) help him, his wife and children for a piece of bread from His Royal Majesty and the Crown.«

HERR HENRIC FLEMING *til Lectis*
Ekeby, Ifenhoft *Fagernäs och Lais m.m.*
Landshöfdinge i Jngerm, *Ståthållare på Narva*
Krigs Öfwerste i Finland, *Vice Amir. och Krigs Råd.*
LANDTMARSKALK *twå gånger 1643 och 1644.*
Född 1584 d. 15. Aug. *Död 1650 d. 7. Nov.*

Ahret Sc.

**Field Marshal and Admiral Henrik Fleming (1584–1650)
is the author of the instructions for the Navy quoted here.**

When the Vasa was placed in her pontoon house at the Wasa Shipyard,
it was a question of keeping the ship's timbers damp with high humidity,
a prerequisite for succeeding with preservation with polyglycol.

A DIFFERENT CONSERVATION

ALTHOUGH the hull of the Vasa was in surprisingly good condition after three centuries at the bottom of Strömmen, it would not remain so if allowed to dry out without any further treatment. This constituted a conservation problem that quite literally was greater than anything else concerned with organic material. The huge hull alone contained about 900 cubic metres of sodden timber, mainly oak. Added to that were about 12,000 constructional parts of the ship, 700 sculptures and carved details, and more than 12,000 objects in wood, textiles, leather, glass, ceramics and metal that had been part of the equipment of the ship and her crew. Six of the Vasa's original ten sails had also been found in a sail store on board, all very fragile and in a poor state.

The problems were great and no ready solutions available. There was plenty of good advice, but in this important context, the only reliable aids were the results of all the laboratory experiments that had been feverishly underway. Loose articles could be put into water until further notice. On the other hand, the hull required selecting an effective and reliable treatment as soon as possible. From the very beginning, it had been a matter of urgency to bring to the Vasa project experts as advisers within any professional field that might be necessary when it came to conservation.

The Vasa pontoon superstructure was ready in good time before the winter cold came in 1961, and in a position to receive the ship in an acceptable climate. Then it was possible to carry out the final clearing of all the spaces between the inner and outer planking that had hitherto been inaccessible.

As good as the entire hull and the majority of all the carvings are of oak, other items mostly of linden and pine. Best preserved is of course the heartwood oak which is not attacked as easily as softer kinds of timber. From their long spell under water, the timbers contained a very large quantity of water. Typical figures are 1.5 kilos water for every kilo of oak timber, 2 kilos when it comes lime wood. When the Vasa oak dries, it can shrink twice as much as green oak. Reducing or at best eliminating this shrinking – to acquire a stabilisation of dimension – was the aim of the conservation. But how was this to be achieved?

Eventually it was decided that it would be best to try to find a preparation that was dissoluble in water and could be »carried« into the timber by all the water that was stored there. In its turn, this meant that at all costs the Vasa was not to be allowed to dry out too quickly. The solution became the installation of a sprinkler system in the pontoon house. This was of a dimension that it could hold 95–98% of relative air moisture in the building, i.e. just at dew point.

One substance that particularly interested the conservation experts round the Vasa was polyethyleneglycol (PEG), an oil product also used in such items as lipstick, handcreams and baking powder. A method of using PEG to conserve timber had been invented by Rolf Morén and Bertil Centerwall. This method, patented by Mo & Domsjö AB in 1952, was benevolently put at the Vasa project's disposal. Laboratory experiments soon showed that this was practicable. Thus there was access to the stabilisation of dimension part of the desired preparation. In order also to have complete protection from decay, boracic acid and borax were selected to be added to the PEG solution.

From expert quarters, it was stated in all seriousness at an early stage that it would be best to dismantle the whole ship into its separate parts and conserve them in containers. After that, they were to be re-assembled and complemented with the parts that had been torn away or had loosened from the ship. Had that actually been done, it is unlikely that it would ever have been possible to put the bits of the puzzle together again into a whole ship. Changes in shape in connection with conservation were in fact one of the more difficult problems to solve. So it has undeniably been preferable that as much as possible of primarily steamed and curved parts of the ship be conserved in their positions in the hull and in the form they were to have in future.

There were probably many who had doubts about whether it would be possible to succeed in conserving on this mammoth scale. Nonetheless, in April 1962 the treatment of the Vasa's hull began according to the PEG method. From a mixing tank on land, the conservation solution was pumped out to the ship in the pontoon house through a system of pipes. Inside and outside the hull, four men in black rub-

In the sail store on board were the six sails that had not been set when the Vasa sailed. The fragile remains of the sails had to be handled under water when they were unfolded and the pieces put together like a puzzle.

About 600 square metres of sail was found on board. This is a piece of the mizzen's bonnet.

ber suits and white helmets could be seen climbing around and carefully spraying the ship with long mouthpieces, each treatment taking about five hours. In September 1962, it was estimated that the four men had sprayed 90 tons of conservation fluid over the hull.

The atmosphere in the pontoon house was dense. Not only could the men spraying with their hissing mouthpieces be seen spreading polyglycol mist over the ship, but also the air-moisturising apparatus was kept going at the desired level to maintain the moisture in the air. The mist was often as dense as it had once been round King Gustav II Adolf's camp before the battle of Lützen. In many ways this was troublesome for spectators, who found it difficult to see the whole ship.

When an automatic spraying system with fixed spray-nozzles was installed in 1965, this meant that at a reasonable cost, the treatment could be intensified. The apparatus was built up round a central system of pipes to which about 500 spray-nozzles were attached and distributed evenly over the ship both internally and externally. With the help of automation, intensive spraying of the hull could be afforded with short intervals day and night (spraying for 25 minutes, pause for 20 minutes, spraying for 25 minutes and so on). But naturally the ship could not absorb such large quantities of fluid, so in order not to waste expensive conservation material, a central tank was arranged beneath the middle of the ship down in the pontoon. From there, the fluid was pumped via base pipes out to all the spray-nozzles, which finally distributed it in a fine spray both inside and outside the ship. All surplus fluid trickling over the ship ran back into the central tank, to be used once again. Now that the hull was being constantly washed over with fluid, it was no longer necessary to use the old air-moisturising system, and the mist was also disposed of.

The effectiveness of the automatic system very soon showed itself. After only a year, the ship had absorbed roughly twice as much conservation substance as it had over the three previous years. Naturally it was necessary to keep the whole of this process under control, so about 100 bore-samples were regularly taken from various parts of the ship. Via analyses of these timber it was possible to follow how much PEG and borax the Vasa had absorbed. At the turn of the year 1965–66, it was possible to see with some satisfaction the whole of the outer planking, the huge ribs and the inner trimming with a combined thickness of about 45 centimetres had been penetrated by the conservation fluid – still too low a concentration, but the method was clearly working. The borax, which penetrated the timber more easily than PEG, had at this point already been absorbed in sufficient quantities. Considering that the ship is mainly built of mature oak, this was a very good result.

Many of the hundreds of barrels found on board were smashed during the disaster, but some remained whole and were stored in water awaiting conservation.

Vulnerable wooden objects such as this beer bottle turned in birchwood have been preserved by freeze-drying.

From many points of view, it was a great relief when the planned conservation programme turned out to hold and this first phase in the stages of conservation – intensive spraying – could be finished in the spring of 1972. The carpenters now no longer needed to take advantage of breaks in the spraying, and could work and move freely all day on and inside the ship. But with this, the treatment of the hull was not entirely complete, and the follow-up treatment entailed saturating the outer surface of the timber with PEG for as long as possible. The spraying was done every night, and it was also important to regulate the now introduced course of drying to the desired pace.

From the start, the Vasa timbers had a moisture quotient of 150%, which means that every kilo of dry timber held 1.5 kilos water. Despite the fact that the moisture in the pontoon house was kept at up to 95%, gradually, bit by bit, the Vasa was slowly drying out. By 1969, the moisture quotient had fallen to 100%, which meant the Vasa held as much water as dry timber. The final desired result for drying was a moisture quotient of about 20%, which meant that the Vasa would then have evaporated 500 tons of water. In November 1977, the moisture quotient was down to 42% and by 1979, drying had gone so far that spraying could cease completely. With that, the introduced drying process could continue into its final phase up to a state of equilibrium.

The method described here of spraying polyglycol solution over the ship is not the very best if a swift and effective penetration is required. On the other hand, it was the only practicable one possible in view of the size of the ship. Otherwise, the ideal is conservation in closed containers, in which temperature and concentration can be kept under constant control. In the large and well-equipped conservation installation built in connection with the salvaging, in order to deal with the tens of thousands of objects the archaeologists and divers had brought ashore, two 20 metre long containers were mounted, together containing 80 cubic metres. In them, very large constructional parts of the ship could be treated, large beams, for instance, and long planks.

The finds to be conserved were stowed in these containers with great care, if at all possible stowing the same kinds of timber together, for the length of conservation time is longer for oak than for softer timbers. When the container was fully stowed, it was first filled with clean water and the temperature raised to 65 degrees. Then the protective anti-decay solution was added, a 2% solution of boracic acid and borax. After that came the turn of the polyglycol. So that absorbtion into the timber should be as high as possible, the concentration was increased very slowly, during the first months by only 1/12% per twenty-four hours. When that period was over, the pace was increased. Over five months, 1/5% was added per twenty-four hours and the whole process ended with 1/2% per twenty-four hours over the last month.

After eighteen months, the PEG concentration was up to 60%. The conservation bath was complete and the container could be unpacked. Over an almost equal period of time, the timbers slowly dried out with constant surface treatment with PEG. The surplus PEG on the surface was finally melted away with warm air for the timber to have a durable and attractive surface. The last container of Vasa finds was emptied of its contents of blocks, mermaids and parts of barrels and casks in May, 1977.

Among the many wooden objects salvaged from the Vasa were also some that could be regarded as more difficult to conserve than others. Primarily, these were wooden spoons, turned bowls, jars and bottles and other objects made of very soft and hydrous wood. Another method called freeze-drying was chosen for these. The technique has long been used within the food and pharmaceutical industries, but has also turned out to be suitable for use in conservation contexts for vulnerable museum artefacts made of organic materials. The freeze-drying technique is based on the fact that ice, placed under a vacuum, turns from firm form to gas form without passing the liquid form. Leather articles, for instance, can also be treated very advantageously with this method.

Many objects made of other materials also had to be treated to preserve them. The never-used cannon balls were still on board. In contrast to wrought iron, the cast iron had not rusted away, but had been affected by its long period in the water. When the archaeologists started bringing up the cannon balls, they found to their surprise that equal-sized balls sometimes weighed over ten kilos and sometimes hardly a kilo. The reason why the cast iron retained its form although most of the iron had sometimes disappeared is that it had originally had a much higher carbon content than the wrought iron. If a cannon ball that had lain in the water for a long time is brought up into the air, the rusting continues very quickly and the ball disintegrates from within.

The method chosen to preserve iron objects is reduction, entailing them being heated up in a specially constructed furnace in a hydrogen gas atmosphere up to about 1,000 degrees, thus reducing the rust, and the original iron being re-formed.

Three of the Vasa's large bower anchors were salvaged during the last stage of the diving. No furnaces exist for such large iron objects, so instead they had to take to old and tried mechanical methods to get rid of the rust – brushing, sandblasting and painting with rust preventative.

A real challenge for the conservation staff came with the sails found on board. It was presumed from the start that a number of reserve sails had been found in the sail store on the orlop deck. However, it eventually turned out to be a part of the set of sails which had not been used when the Vasa began sailing. According to information, they had then set four sails: foresail, foretopsail, main topsail and mizzen. That corresponds very well, going by what was found in the sail store, where the rest of the Vasa's ten sails were kept folded up; spritsail and upper spritsail, fore topgallant, main sail, main topgallant and mizzen topsail. The sail store also contained a bonnett for the mizzen and a set of sails for the longboat.

Two types of textile fibres were distinguishable before the days of synthetic fibres – animal and vegetable. Animal fibres tolerate soaking in water well, vegetable fibres do not. All sails are made of vegetable fibres and so are very damaged. It is very difficult to define whether they are made of flax or hemp, as even when new these fibres are similar. However, analyses indicated that the sails were made of hemp.

Unfolding that number of sails in which the canvas was no longer capable of bearing its own weight has been an almost insuperable problem. The same applies to the question of how to put the puzzle bits together and mount them so that they can be preserved for the future. So that the fragile pieces of sail should not crumble away when unfolded, the work had to be done under water in large flat containers. The cleaning was done with detergent in the water, then the water replaced by clean ethyl-alcohol, which then in its turn was replaced with toluol. After that procedure, it was possible to dry out the pieces of sail without risk.

The puzzle of the cleaned and dried pieces of sail was put together on a fibreglass cloth in 2 × 2 metre squares. A special plastic produced at the conservation laboratory was then used to bind the sails to the fibreglass cloth, its covering layers protecting them against the damaging effect of the air. The plastic, painted on, has the same light-breaking index as the fibreglass, which means that the originally white fibreglass becomes transparent when the plastic layer is applied. With the sail canvas protected in this way, the squares of canvas could then be kept in store. For exhibition, the squares containing the Vasa's smallest sail, the fore topgallant, have been joined together. The 32 square metre sail can be seen at the Vasa Museum – almost certainly the oldest preserved sail in the world.

Using this method of preserving the original sails did not mean anything irretrievable had been done. Should anyone for some reason not be satisfied with the mounting, it is possible to dissolve the plastic with toluol. Sorting out and conserving the sails has been a very time-consuming and difficult task. Nor is this a matter of a few small canvases, as almost 600 square metres in all have been prepared.

Conservation problems are often difficult to solve. When it came to the Vasa and the Vasa material, the problems have been particularly troublesome as they have concerned water-saturated timbers in huge volumes. Even where there have been traditional treatments to turn to, possibilities of finding even better methods have been investigated. The Vasa Museum has had great support from the Conservation Council once organised by the Wasa Commission. Apart from representatives of the museum, the council also has had on it leading scientists and specialists within their actual subject fields. The council has in its turn worked entirely voluntarily and been invaluable support to the management of the museum.

The conservation of the Vasa has meant making a great many, sometimes difficult judgements and decisions, not least, it turned out, in 1976–77 when the question of the final treatment of the ship became a government issue. The decision to cease all spraying, taken by the museum board, was based on recommendations by the council of experts. The head of the museum conservation department held another view and went to the government to have the museum management's decision upheld. The result, however, was that the government announced its confidence in the action of the museum board.

The major concentration on various kinds of conservation matters has been a necessary prerequisite for the Vasa project. Naturally enough it has aroused great international interest, and leading specialists from various parts of the world have studied the work carried out by the Vasa Museum's conservation department.

**Replacing the lower standing rigging was the final phase
in the restoration of the Vasa. This is the main mast being lifted into place.**

OPERATION VASA REDIVIVA

ONCE the archaeologists had carried out the vital excavations of the interior of the Vasa and the hull had been emptied and cleaned of sediment and dirt, it was time to begin on the next great adventure – rebuilding the ship. The hull was largely in good condition despite its 333 years on the sea bed, but several vital parts had nevertheless fared rather badly in the depths. Nails and bolts had rusted away, so the beakhead, the sterncastle and quarter galleries had collapsed. In 1962, they were all simply heaps of loose parts in the silt round the hollow the Vasa had left behind her after she had been brought up.

Most of the sculptures and ornamental carving that had once been the magnificent adornment of the royal ship had suffered the same fate. Nails and bolts that had held them in place on the ship had rusted away and the sculptures had loosened and fallen, some inside, but most into the clay and mud outside the ship. Of the rigging, all that could be seen was the broken-off lower parts of the main mast and foremast. The mizzen mast had completely disappeared.

Unfortunately, the site of the wreck was just where many other ships often used to anchor, which was also why the Vasa had suffered considerable damage. It can also be presumed that the many attempts during the seventeenth century to salvage the ship or its equipment had not gone by totally without trace. Of the Vasa's 64 guns, only three were left, and nearly all the planking on the upper deck had gone as a result of these salvage operations.

When the Vasa was raised, most of the loose finds on the sea bed round the ship were left to their fate. But they also had to be salvaged in order to have access to as much original material as possible when restoration was to begin. So in 1963, diving with civilian and naval divers co-operating, was started again under the direction of the experienced chief diver Fälting. It took five summer seasons to clean up the area round and inside the hollow the Vasa had left in the clay.

About 15,000 cubic metres of silt was sucked up to the surface, where it was sieved for minor finds, while a constant stream of larger pieces were sent up by the divers. When, as far as could be judged, the site had been emptied of finds, the divers had searched through and sieved sediment over an area 100 metres long and 40 metres wide. As an extra measure, they also made a number of 15–20 metre long shafts outside this area, in directions considered conceivable that ships dropping anchor might have dragged with them and dropped pieces of the Vasa's superstructure.

By November 1967, the time had at last come to put a stop to diving. For a festive finale, a couple of major final liftings were made for the press, radio and television. Again the pontoon crane, the *Lodbrok*, was brought into service and as a grand finale raised what was almost certainly the Vasa's longboat. This is a 12 metre long, 3 metre wide boat of very sturdy construction, built in the Dutch manner with a flat bottom and an external nailed-on keel, intended to be rowed by eight pairs of oars, but could also be sailed, for which it was equipped with swords on the sides. It also has a transverse brake windlass as well as a sheave in its stem.

The longboat was found just before the question of ceasing operations had been considered. During the early stages before, when the divers were making the cable tunnels underneath the Vasa, they had come across another somewhat smaller boat, which had almost certainly been crushed when the Vasa was twisted out of her hollow at the first lift. Various parts of it have been brought up, however, and eventually perhaps there will be enough pieces for it also to be put together again. Apart from some ballast stones, inside the salvaged longboat were some pieces of rigging that had come free from the Vasa and fallen down into it.

With roughly 12,000 loose constructional parts and about 700 sculptures and carvings to put together with the hull into as whole a ship as possible, it was fairly natural that the restoration work soon came to be called the largest jigsaw-puzzle in the world. And a puzzle it has been. A great many pieces quickly and obviously fell into their given places, but the majority demanded not only a great ability to observe and combine, but also considerable powers of deduction to be able to complete the complicated jigsaw-puzzle, a matter of finding the place and function of thousands of bits of building material of varying sizes and shapes, often quite anonymous.

To start with, there had probably been some idea that restoration work would

The main top was situated just below the upperend of the lower mast of the main mast about 15 metres above deck and was both a working and a battle platform.

Before the diving was completed, the Vasa's 12 metre long longboat was salvaged.

primarily be solved and guided from desks and drawing boards, from which it would be possible to calculate how the many parts had once hung together, after which the carpenters would then put them in place on the ship. The reality became something quite different, of course. Skilled carpenters under the direction of Johan Blomman, eventually succeeded by Göran Näsvall and most recently Ossi Gröndal, have identified the pieces and seen to their placing in the ship. Parallel to this, their work was followed up with drawings and sketches recording the solutions they had come to. A specialist in ship drawings, Eva-Marie Stolt, has been working all the time on producing blueprints of the ship which the seventeenth century shipbuilders never achieved.

Naturally some good restoration results can be achieved the »desk« way, which has also been tried with some success. By measuring a certain category of objects in a mould-bench in combination with studies of contact surfaces and nail holes in the hull, it was possible to reconstruct in drawing form one of the quarter galleries, which turned out to have the extended form with a tower at both ends characteristic of contemporary Dutch shipbuilding.

The most advanced example of a reconstruction done the drawing board way is the outstandingly fine rigging reconstruction carried out by Eva-Marie Stolt. With a starting point in the preserved masts, attachment details in the hull of the Vasa, the salvaged sails and diverse preserved cordage remains, deadeyes and blocks found, contemporary literature and pictures, she has provided a complete and largely accurate picture of what the Vasa's rigging looked like in detail.

Once the restoration work had started and the carpenters had begun first searching, then fitting in the found parts directly on to and into the hull, the work turned out to progress quite quickly. There were several starting points from which the various problems could be approached. In the hull were many traces in the form of nail holes, bolt holes and contact marks which it was a matter of interpreting correctly. In many cases, the special form and construction of the ship did not allow more than one interpretation when it came to replacing a certain constructional element.

Almost all additions to the hull – the beakhead, the sterncastle, galleries, ornamentation etc – had been fastened with nails hammered in with no particular system. This meant the nail holes formed individual patterns at every attachment. When a combination of nail holes had been sought out by inserting a simple steel-probe, it provided an unambiguous answer to whether a certain piece of wood was to sit in just that place or not.

The numerous sculptures also played a certain part in the interpretation of the

**The 10.3 metre high and 3 ton heavy rudder is lifted
into the Wasa shipyard to be conveyed to the ship.**

ship's construction. The majority had only exceptionally had a bearing or directly supporting function. On the other hand, they had been carved to suit a certain base wherever they were to be attached. So the backs of the sculptures fairly well reflected the shape of the base.

All the nails and bolts had rusted away during the time the Vasa had been on the sea bed, but when she was being built, fortunately both iron bolts and wooden nails were used. About 40 treenails per square metre in the sides of the ship meant that the hull was very strong, although the iron bolts had gone. The tough wooden bindings allowed a certain amount of movement in the hull, so the hull was presumably slightly deformed at the first docking, as huge quantities of silt still remained inside the ship. The ship's sides had thus been pressed down by this abnormally large internal burden, with the consequence that many of the hull's connections had been displaced so that it proved impossible to fit new bolts into the old holes. However, it was very necessary to replace the vanished bolting with new bolts to make the hull quite stable again and to secure its form.

To achieve this, the provisional shoring first had to be replaced by something more stable and permanent. So a tailor-made supporting cradle of steel was ordered from Kockums in Malmö, and in this the Vasa would rest. This cradle, 45 metres long and weighing 19 tons, was installed in the autumn of 1964. Once in place, it formed a stable foundation that made it possible to set about straightening up the hull.

The task turned out to be lengthy and laborious, with no real visible elements that might interest the public. On the other hand, for the restoration team it was not only exciting, but also absolutely necessary as the first stage in the re-building work. With about fifteen jacks in combination with wedges inserted between the cradle and the hull, slowly but surely, the carpenters pressed the ship's sides up again. Round and round the hull they went with the jacks, gaining millimetre by millimetre. It took about six months, but their labours paid off, the deformation was reversed, anyhow far enough so that the bolt holes were now open again. The ship could now be bolted with about 4,000 newly manufactured bolts from 70 up to 230 centimetres long.

At the same time it was also possible to undertake a few other adjustments. Between the stern and the aft end of the planking was a large gap. Now that the sides of the hull had been adjusted up, the major part of this space was retrieved. By simply lifting slightly under the stern end of the keel, so that the stern tipped into the correct position, the gap was closed.

The planking along the stem had loosened in the rabbet and there was a gap of

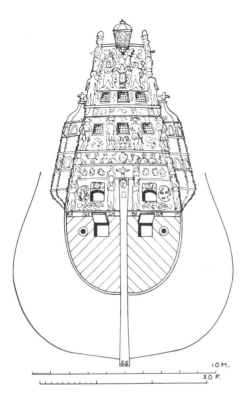

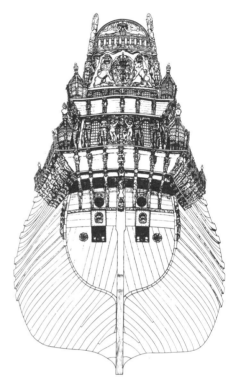

During the first stage of the salvaging, when there were only vague ideas of the ship's appearance, Captain Sam Svensson tried to imagine what the ship might have looked like. The reality has widely surpassed his imagination.
Drawing by Gunnar Olofsson.

Instead of a name-board on the stern, the name of the Vasa is represented by the Vasa family coat-of-arms. The colouring is done in strong colours with elements of gilding, which is shown here on a painted cast of the original.

about 1 1/2 inches. This gap was also closed with the help of jacks and draught-rod so that only normal caulking distance was left. At the same time the front part of the keel was raised to its original place, as it had been lying slightly pressed down in the keel-blocks.

Parallel with all this utterly necessary basic work so that the real re-building of the ship could begin, starting out from all the loose constructional parts, an attempt was made to create a picture of the original appearance of the Vasa. Naturally, the centre of interest lay in the ruined sterncastle. Pieces of the puzzle soon began to fit in here and there. That was when the sculptures came to play an important part. Hans Soop, the museum art historian, concentrated on interpreting the sculpture material, primarily those which in such a rich measure had their places on the sterncastle.

The crown of the stern, a large bow-shaped group of sculptures, provided information on the sterncastle's greatest width at its highest point. By drawing out the ship's falling-in side lines, which were marked by the deck widths astern and which the remaining hull sides showed, it was possible to place the crown at roughly the correct height and acquire a grasp of the form and size of the sterncastle. Bit by bit, the assembly of sculptures belonging in the Vasa's stern increased as the divers continued to work on the site, providing increased nourishment to the composition. One of the two long corner pillars that had once framed the upper part of the sterncastle was also found, and that provided some new measurement references.

The great national coat-of-arms, which turned out to have had its place below the stern crown, was of central importance to the picture of the sterncastle's appearance. This find in particular can also serve as an illustration of how thorough the search of the find area on the bottom of Strömmen had been. Over years of diving, scattered pieces of the national coat-of-arms had been brought to the surface, and with 22 individual parts found, this magnificent piece of carving was again complete, all except an earshell ornament at the paw of one of the lions.

By 1965, the work of righting, stabilising and bolting the Vasa's hull was at last at an end and the real re-building could begin. Nearly all the planking belonging to the flat stern could be brought out and put in place, as well as the many strong stern beams that had been nearest above the flat stern. But then there was a sudden stop. The upper stern beam was missing from the finds, so the work on the sterncastle was left for the time being.

Restoration work in 1966 was begun by the carpenters replacing the great deck beams with their huge self-grown timber knees on the badly damaged upper deck. The majority of the planks up there were missing, a result of the work of Hans

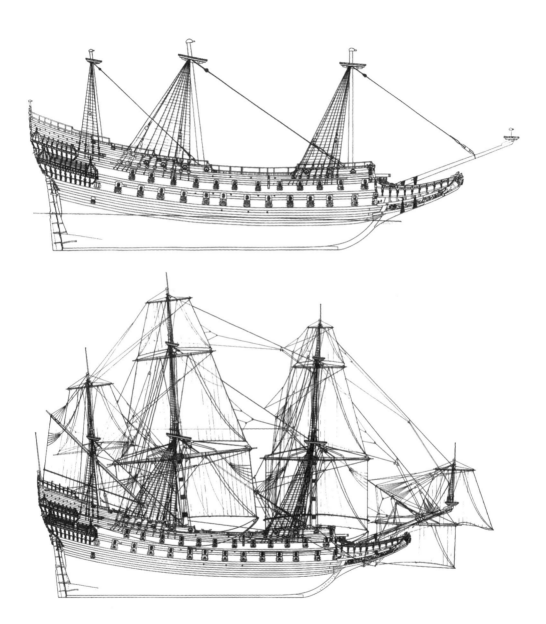

**The aim of the restoration of the Vasa was to reconstruct the ship
as she looked in winter with her topmasts, topgallant masts and running
rigging in store and only the lower standing rigging up.
Fully rigged, the ship had ten sails.** Drawing by Eva-Marie Stolt.

Albecht von Treileben and his divers in the seventeenth century. The majority of the beams had been torn from their original places, but were still inside the ship. However, many were broken or cracked, so had to be reinforced. This was done in a simple and effective way. With a chainsaw, a long slit was sawn down the middle line along the top length of the beam and a blade of stainless steel inserted into it. Transverse bolts were inserted wherever there was a break, and when new deck planks were eventually to be laid on the upper deck, they would cover both the sawn slot and the steel reinforcement. The last element in the work at this stage was putting back the waterways planks and when that was done, activities were moved over to the beakhead.

Work on the beakhead rapidly produced results. Four strong knees which were to hold the beakhead to the stem were mounted. The central support piece·of the bowsprit , joists and ribs could be put in place. A picture of what the Vasa's forebody had looked like began to emerge when the bulging blunt bow of the hull was hidden by the slim and long protruding great beakhead. But the design of the forebody was given yet another important complement. It turned out that a turned bulkhead had covered the hitherto open part towards the upper battery deck. In this bulkhead were two ports with bow-shaped upper pieces, and through these the crew could via a few steps get down into the beakhead. The benches for belaying pins there confirm that the beakhead was an important working platform. From there were manoeuvered the square sails, called spritsail and upper spritsail, farthest out on the bowsprit. In addition there might have been other urgent needs that meant a man had to make his way out there. That was where the crew had to manage their personal needs. The toilets – two in number – consisted of simple square wooden drums with seats on top.

As the restoration work progressed, it became increasingly clear that the size of the Vasa had been misjudged when the pontoon house had been measured and constructed, an understandable mistake. All they had to go by were the measurements made of the hull as it lay on the sea bed, and time was short, as was access to money. The dry dock's dimensions had also meant certain limitations to the size of the pontoon. Naturally it was very irritating to have to break off the work on the beakhead. But calculations now made possible showed that the nose of the figurehead lion would end up about five metres outside the gable wall of the pontoon house. In principle, the appearance of the beakhead was known. Most of the pieces of the puzzle were to hand, but until further notice, the mounting of them could not continue for reasons of space.

Instead, work was concentrated on the ship's sides, where all the railing supports

**The lower-cap of the main mast is lifted into place.
It serves as an attachment for the central part of the mast, the topmast.**

could be put back in their original places. A number of filling pieces that were to go between the supports could be identified and their situations defined, and with those in place, the sixteen round gun-ports that had been on the upper deck were also brought out. With that, the hull silhouette from the forebody to the beginning of the sterncastle began to be clearly distinguishable.

Discussions on the continued building up of the sterncastle had gone on. These also concerned the placing of the aforementioned quarter galleries. Previously, ships had had open balconies round the sterncastle, where bowmen, cross-bowmen or musketeers could be placed for close combat. By the time the Vasa was built, the galleries, according to the Dutch manner, were covered, cramped inside, and outside supplied with a wealth of carved decoration – decorative elements with no particular practical function. Particularly remarkable in the Vasa's case is that she had two galleries on each side, one above the other, something no one had ever seen anything like before on paintings or drawings from the same period. The lower galleries had completing towers at both ends, while the smaller upper galleries had only one stern tower. This is where the only tangible use for the quarter galleries can be found – in the stern towers, a deck is inserted and that was probably the place where the tubs serving as the officers' toilets were placed.

One thing was certain. The Vasa had quite different dimensions from what had been thought at the start. Not only would the beakhead protrude far outside the forebody gable wall, it was now clear that the sterncastle would jut out in two stages and would thus end up outside the stern gable wall of the pontoon house. In addition to that, the sterncastle was considerably higher than had been calculated, so the roof of the building would have to be raised above the stern.

All that could be done now was to establish that the restoration work could go no further with the available space in the pontoon house. It was true the National Board of Public Building had begun to investigate finding a suitable building site for the permanent Vasa Museum that would have to be provided, but considering the time it would take to provide a finished building, even if the whole process could be started at once and continue without disturbance, the provisional protective building would have to be added to so that the restoration could be completed.

Another problem arose in this context. The Vasa in its pontoon house was floating on a concrete pontoon. By then, the restoration work had already meant that a previously decided safety margin of at least 50 centimetres freeboard had been passed. So it was necessary somehow to increase the bearing strength of the pontoon. To that end, two concrete pontoons were constructed and laid one on each side of the Vasa pontoon. These extra floating elements had a protruding heel down below along the entire long side. The heel gripped under the main pontoon, and the new pontoons were joined and held in place with the aid of bracing stays running under the bottom of the old pontoon. With the aid of this extra floating strength, it was possible to keep an even freeboard with a good margin of safety.

When the re-building of the pontoon house began, it was necessary to keep the air moisture as level as possible while the work was going on. The added buildings at the gable ends were constructed outside the old walls, which were not taken down until the new ones were complete. The greatest problem from a climate point of view was raising the roof over the sterncastle. There was nothing else for it but have the builders build a provisional inner roof over that part of the ship.

The most exciting phase in the rebuilding work came when two of the very large concrete beams right across the ship up below the roof had to be sawn free from their spans and lifted out after they had been supplied with new, higher arch-constructions of steel. If one of those concrete colossi had been dropped, presumably the entire stern part of the Vasa would have been crushed. The re-building was completed by the turn of the year 1968–69. Now there was sufficient space to complete the restoration, though with one exception. The return of the rigging and bowsprit had to wait until the Vasa could move to a new permanent museum.

With renewed strength, the team of carpenters could again take up their interrupted work on the beakhead after the new year of 1969. Bit by bit, the puzzle was being completed. There were to be nine pairs of ribs, eighteen ribs, each one of which had been decorated with a Roman emperor. A few pieces were missing, among them the lower long beam of the beakhead running from the stem right up to the place for the figurehead lion. The beakhead was otherwise so complete that there was no difficulty reconstructing the form and dimensions of the beam and making a new one. With the delight of this successful result, to crown the work, though only provisionally, a cast of the Vasa's figurehead lion was placed farthest out on the beakhead.

The time then came to return to the stern, knowledge of which had by now been considerably clarified, not least owing to the exhibition called »The Power and the Glory« that had attracted great attention and was opened in the Wasa Shipyard premises in the spring of 1968. Hans Soop, the art historian, had long been working to find the sculpture plan that had guided the decorating of the Vasa's sterncastle. For the first time in modern times, the main part of the warship's magnificent ornamentation was displayed at this exhibition. The centrepiece of the exhibition was a horizontally laid copy of the almost 20 metre high stern, on which Hans Soop and the carpenters together had put all the original sculptures. And happily enough, it was now confirmed that the imagined concept of the sterncastle's design was largely correct. The entire sculpture plan of the stern could be fitted in on to the exhibition dummy with the symbol of her name, the Vasa dynasty's coat-of-arms and the great national coat-of-arms as central motifs. The calculated measurements proved correct.

However, the time had not yet come to continue with the building up of the sterncastle. It had been realised that as it would be so high and had been so broken up, something radical had to be done to reinforce the bearing strength of the construction. One possibility – the simplest – would be to make a complementary outer shoring astern of the ship. As everyone was in agreement that that was a far too clumsy solution, instead it was decided to have a shoring-construction made of stainless steel with strong U-girders that could be laid into the sides of the hull and linked internally with transverse steel plates along the stern. So as not to spoil the appearance of the hull, a strake of the planking was taken out when the girders were to be inserted. The girders were fixed in, the planks thinned to the thickness of the girders, after which the planks were put back again so that they covered the whole body of the girders. Extra bearing strength of that kind was built in at both the lower and upper gallery levels.

During 1970, the bearing parts of the sterncastle were built up to full height and the various decks of the sterncastle began to be fitted in, the three ton rudder also put in place. However, this could not be done until all the rusted-away wrought-iron fittings had been replaced with some newly-made to hold it in place. Only the lowest gudgeon on the stern stem remained, as it had been pressed down in the mud, so had escaped destruction. No steering wheel existed in the Vasa's day. Her rudder was manoeuvered with the aid of a vertical whipstaff passing through the deck in the steerage to the fore of the main cabin. Below the deck, it was attached to the 9.5 metre long tiller, which in its turn was fastened to the top of the rudder. A reserve tiller was also found during the excavation of the Vasa's orlop deck.

Attention should now be drawn to the Vasa's decoration, as the magnificent decor of the royal ship was so essential. Today, it may appear that unreasonable expense and labour had been expended on the ornamentation of the ship, but that was all in the spirit of the day. The French Minister of Finance, Jean-Baptiste Colbert has summarised his view in one sentence: »Nothing could be more impressive, nor more devoted to glorifying His Majesty than that his ship bears the most magnificent ornamentation ever seen on the high seas.«

Power with consequent splendour and glory have always had a high status, slicing through the epochs, and this certainly does not apply only to worldly power.

Beneath each of the Vasa's two cathead beams is a male figure,
apparently a Pole, in a degrading position. According to Polish tradition,
a nobleman who had behaved basely was to crawl before his equals
in under a bench and bark like a dog. By humiliating himself before others,
he could be forgiven and received back into his circle.
This is psychological warfare – a humiliated opponent from
the arch-enemy Poland placed in the forebody of a Swedish warship.

The ornamentation of the Vasa has fully shown itself to correspond to the content of Colbert's words on the splendidly ornamented ship as the best status symbol for the power of the monarch – and for that matter of the realm. A floating wooden palace shimmering in bright colours and gilt.

The constant stream of sculptures brought up from the depths into the light of day has shown that Swedish ship ornamentation in no way lagged behind that of Dutch and English decor. During the sixteenth century, ships usually had a painted figure on the stern referring to the ship's name. In Sweden, for instance, the ship *Elefanten* in 1599 was decorated with a painted elephant.

Towards the end of the sixteenth century the painted ornamentation gradually began to be replaced by sculptured decor. The roughly 700 sculptures and carved ornaments salvaged from the Vasa provide a clear picture of the impressive splendour of the ship, a throng of figures and motifs from mythology, the Bible and Antiquity, as well as political elements and not least a glorification of the monarch himself, King Gustav II Adolf.

On the whole, all colour had disappeared during the time the sculptures had lain in the water, and at the salvaging only a few individual traces of paint were visible, the remains of gold-leaf glittering here and there, most of all on the mane of the lion in the national coat-of-arms. With the aid of modern techniques, in a research project in the 1990's led by the conservationist Peter Tångeberg, he has nevertheless been able to ascertain fairly well the way the sculptures were painted. Throughout were bright colours with reinforcing elements of gold-leaf, on the sterncastle against a background painted red.

The array of sculptures salvaged from the Vasa is not only interesting as splendid examples of ship adornment from the early seventeenth century, but from a general art history point of view, a find of this size is significant. From an international viewpoint, this is a large collection of profane wooden sculptures from the actual period and which also contains a number of sculptures of a high artistic standard.

The seventeenth century is the century of Baroque in Europe, but up in the Nordic countries a certain lagging behind had been acknowledged, including when it came to cultural currents on the continent. Thus the Vasa's sculptures primarily represent a style of art called German-Dutch Renaissance. But it is clear that Baroque was beginning to come in with certain stylistic features. In the Vasa figures, there is much that is typical of Baroque – the richness of form and movement, the organic and the grandiose.

According to bills from Stockholm shipyard, there were two German and one Dutch master-carvers active during the building of the Vasa – Hans Clausink,

Mårten Redtmer and Johan Didrichson Tijssen. To be able to produce so many sculptures during the relatively short period of the building of the ship, it is more than likely that the carvers' labourers did the rougher work, while the master-carvers were responsible for the final artistic design of the figures. The decor plan did not come about by chance. In that respect, a communication from Admiral Claes Fleming in 1632 can be referred to, in which he enquires what the largest of ships being built should be called »so that the carving could be carried out accordingly«.

As Vasa is the name of the royal family, it is perhaps natural that the stern decor reflects the monarch himself, King Gustaf II Adolf. Up in the crown is an image of the king as a young man, framed by two griffins holding the royal crown above his head. This is not least directed at Poland and her King Sigismund, Gustav Adolf's cousin, who was also a contender to the throne of Sweden. Below in a frieze are the letters GARS, standing for Gustavus Adolphus Rex Sueciae. In the field below is the great national coat-of-arms and below that the crowned Vasa sheaf, which is the Vasa family coat-of-arms and the symbol of the Vasa name. There are also figures of Hercules, which would be appropriate to symbolise the king's power and prosperity. Figures have been taken from the Book of Judges in the Bible to symbolise Gideon's victory over the Midianites, a well-founded parallel with Gustaf Adolf's – as was hoped – successful struggle against the Catholic emperor. The Vasa's sculptural splendour and the interesting symbolic language applied by seventeenth century carvers have been the objects of thorough study by Hans Scoop, who described his observations in his doctoral thesis.

During the 1970's, more and more pieces found their way from the huge store to their original places on the ship. Here and there some parts were missing, some pieces of planking, for instance, in the ceiling of the sterncastle. But on the whole, the number of missing original parts was negligible. One guiding principle of the restoration has been to mark clearly where reconstructed and newly manufactured parts have been placed in the puzzle. No attempts to give an »antique« finish to newly-made parts have been made. Instead they have been treated so that they do not clash too badly with the original material, but so that the genuine articles can easy be distinguished from the new parts, and the new parts are few.

Alongside the carpenters' work on restoration, the museum's ship-design expert, Eva Marie Stolt, has recorded the Vasa in the most minutest detail in a first class series of drawings. There is a full set of blueprints at the Vasa museum today – from line drawings to side views, blueprints of decks and rigging and drawings of details etc. Complemented by drawings, sketches and photographs, these blueprints provide a total and very detailed picture of the warship the Vasa. Most difficult of all was the reconstruction of the Vasa's standing and running rigging, which Eva-Marie Stolt worked out in blueprint form from the limited remains of sails and cordage, marks of fastenings in the hull, loose parts from the rigging and intensive studies of the limited comparitive material existing from the period, she has succeeded in producing the greatest credible representation of the Vasa's original rigging. It was to be the foundation for the future rigging of the ship, once there was space to replace the lower standing rigging. But the 6.5 kilometres of cordage of various dimensions calculated to be needed was already purchased from a ropeworks in Hamburg. For the time being, it all remained in store.

One of a total of ten grotesque consol heads that appear to hold up the lower quarter galleries.

On the quarter galleries were rows of Roman warriors in armour. This one, with thick brushed-back moustache, had his place on the lower port side quarter gallery. Painted copy.

**Well packed in insulating material to protect her,
the Vasa made her last voyage on December 6th, 1988,
in through the open end of the almost completed new Vasa Museum.**

TOWARDS HER ULTIMATE DESTINATION

A S THE SALVAGING and excavation of the Vasa was going on, the first and provisional museum for the ship was being planned and constructed. It was named of Wasavarvet (the Wasa Shipyard) to make it quite clear that it was primarily to be regarded as a place of work in which the ship would be rebuilt and preserved. The clearly stated condition was that as a museum, it would be provisional for a limited time, ten years at a maximum. This was the period conservation experts calculated was needed for the »wet« phase of conservation, when the ship was to be sprayed with polyglycol solution.

It had also been calculated that the carpenters would at the same time return the Vasa to her original state to the best of their abilities. Working conditions were troublesome with the moisture and the slippery surfaces in the ship's hull as it was constantly being sprayed, and where the carpenters always had to try to carry out as much of the work and as quickly as possible during the brief pauses between the spraying. But these skilled professionals worked their way slowly but surely ahead in the jigsaw puzzle, and were able to restore bit after bit to their rightful places. The Vasa grew and knowledge of early seventeenth century shipbuilding increased at the same pace.

The agreed provisional period came to an end. But provisional arrangements have a remarkable ability to become more long-lived than had at first been envisaged. The Wasa Shipyard was no exception to this rule, and it was fortunate that despite its provisional character, the building functioned as well as it did. The Wasa Shipyard was not least a very special creation from the point of view of the general public. The visitor to the museum was able to experience at close quarters much of what is otherwise work carried out behind the scenes in a museum. The rebuilding work and conservation continued unabated on an open stage, which was interesting to experience. The Vasa was unique in the world and attracted crowds as no other museum in the country could.

The greatest problem of all with the pontoon house built to protect the Vasa came into view on the day in 1979 when the conservation spraying could be ended for good. As long as spraying continued, it had masked what a bad state the protective aluminium shell really was in. When it dried out inside for the first time, it was soon clear that the building was leaking very badly, the insulation was wretched and there was really no hope of controlling the climate inside. There was some equipment to keep the air moist, but not to de-moisten it. There were heating possibilities, but no way of cooling down the air during hot summer days. Rain and melted snow came in through the roof and walls, and troublesome condensation dripped everywhere. There was no longer any way back. If the future preservation of the Vasa was not to be hazarded, and allow all that investment in salvaging, conserving and restoring her go to waste, then something had to be done about a new building.

The idea of letting the provisional Wasa Shipyard be relieved by a new permanent building had been there from the very start. The site for a new museum of that kind was also decided by the then active Wasa Committee. In a statement in 1958 on the possibilities of salvaging the ship, it was said that when the permanent building for the Vasa was to be built, it should be somewhere in the Galär shipyard area, where at the time the naval shipyard in Stockholm was situated, but plans were afoot to move it out from this central city site to a site in the Stockholm archipelago. But the road from this first idea proved to be both a crooked and a very long one.

For a decade or two, the question of just where the permanent museum should be was brought up over and over again. Suggestions for possible sites in a series of different places by the city's waters and sometimes by waters outside the city were discussed and rejected. In 1969, the planned move of the naval shipyard from the Galär shipyard area was carried out, and with that came an opening in the question of localisation. But there were to be yet more political turns before a solution was finally found.

In December 1981 – twenty years after the raising of the Vasa – the National Board of Public Building was able at last to arrange a Scandinavian architectural competition for the man-of-war at the Galär shipyard. The interest was enormous. When the time limit for the competition was reached in April 1982, no fewer than

384 proposals had been handed in. It became a gigantic, pleasing and very difficult task for the competition jury who were to decide the issue. It ended with the jury being unable to agree, but felt they had to award two first prizes. One went to the Copenhagen architects Johan Fogh and Per Følner and the other to the Stockholm architect, Göran Månsson. As both proposals had been revised in line with criticisms they had received from the jury, the National Board for Public Building decided to go to the government with an application to accept the Swedish proposal.

The decision was constantly delayed, but in January 1987, work could begin on the foundations. By the autumn of 1988, work on the building's concrete frame had come so far that the Vasa had to be taken in to the future museum before the still open gable facing the water was to be closed. On September 4th, the provisional Wasa Shipyard was closed to the public, after having served its purpose for twenty-six years. In it, kings, queens, presidents, admirals, space travellers and almost twelve million people from all over the world had been able to marvel at this ship from 1628 it had contained.

On December 6th, the Vasa, standing on her concrete pontoon and wrapped in a protective cover of mineral-wool, could be towed away on her third and last voyage to her final harbour in the new museum. A gun salute roared out and despite the cloudy and cold grey weather, a great many people had gathered on quays and piers to watch the ship's slow journey from the Wasa Shipyard to the Vasa Museum.

On the museum's part there was a definite desire, despite the current building work, not to exclude summer tourists to Stockholm from the chance of seeing the Vasa. With considerable accommodation and co-operation from the builders, it was possible to arrange for visitors during the summer of 1989 to be piloted to the ship, although she was now lying in the middle of a building site.

After intensive final building work, the Vasa Museum's staff were able to take possession of all the premises in February 1990, and hectic activities began. Now it was a matter of completing the planned first four basic exhibitions and prepare for the ceremonial inauguration of the museum. The moment decided on was approaching rapidly. Then with much festive euphoria and before an impressed public, the Vasa Museum was inaugurated on June 15th, 1990 by His Majesty King Carl XVI Gustaf.

The warship Vasa has no equivalent in the world. She has provided us with the opportunity for the first time to study in detail the way in which a large ship was built in the early seventeenth century. As a record of technical shipbuilding and history of shipping, the Vasa is invaluable. But the ship also has much else to give. All the objects rescued at the salvaging reflect life on board in the miniature society the ship once consisted of. The Vasa must also be looked on as a product of the will of society. Alongside the basic maritime history aspects, it provides space to exhibit in the museum the ship's place in her society, and its economic political, religious, social and cultural life as well as to bring out the people who populated that society.

The Vasa is naturally the museum's most important exhibit. The museum building emphasizes this by placing the Vasa in the centre of the main hall and letting all the other activities group round her at various levels. In the cramped old Wasa Shipyard, the public was always so close to the ship, it was never possible to see the ship as a whole. In the great hall of the Vasa Museum, the ship can be seen both at a distance and close to. Through her size, the Vasa is a very tangible presence wherever the visitor is in the museum's exhibitions and other public spaces. The ship lies in the building with her waterline at the entrance level, but the visitor can also go below the ship and be impressed by the ample underwater body or go up to the sterncastle's highest point with its wealth of ornamental sculptures.

For obvius reasons it has been impossible to find space for the ship's entire rigging in the new Vasa museum. The main mast once rose 52 metres above the keel. The reconstructed lower rigging does constitute only a part of the total rigging, but it nevertheless provides a good idea of the relationship between rigging and hull. But an indication of the actual size of the rigging can already be seen when looking at the stylised masts on the roof of the museum building. They have the correct dimensions and show the format of the rigging as it would have been if the Vasa had been lying at the quay.

The visitor can acquire more understanding of what the ship looked like from the magnificent fully-rigged model in the museum which shows the Vasa on a scale of 1:10. The model was made in public from 1986 to 1990 by the National Maritime Museum's modelmakers under the leadership of the skilled model curator, Göran Forss. In terms of quality, the model can be compared favourably with the exquisite models displayed by Master Shipbuilder af Chapman in the eighteenth century. The Vasa model is placed so that the visitor is able to compare it directly with the present preserved and restored Vasa. It provides a vision of the ship which sailed out on to the waters of Strömmen on August 10th, 1628.

Since the ship has been in her permanent museum, she has changed in appearance quite considerably. There was now space to return the lower standing rigging. The Rigging Master, Olof Pipping, with a number of apprentices and in collaboration with the Vasa's carpenters led by Ossi Gröndahl, has taken as his starting point Eva-Marie Stolt's rigging construction. This turned out to be very advanced work, demanding considerable craftsmanship and a goodly portion of parallel

In the museum, the Vasa lies with her standing lower rigging replaced.
Here it is possible to see the ship at a distance and close to,
from the keel to the highest part of the sterncastle.